MW01297855

ORDINARY LIFE, EXTRAORDINARY GOD!

Lessons from Everyday Experiences

HELEN MCCORMACK

WESTBOW
PRESS®
A DIVISION OF THOMAS NELSON
& ZONDERVAN

WestBow Press books may be ordered through booksellers or by contacting:

WestBow Press
A Division of Thomas Nelson & Zondervan
1663 Liberty Drive
Bloomington, IN 47403
www.westbowpress.com
1 (866) 928-1240

Because of the dynamic nature of the Internet, any web addresses or
links contained in this book may have changed since publication and
may no longer be valid. The views expressed in this work are solely those
of the author and do not necessarily reflect the views of the publisher,
and the publisher hereby disclaims any responsibility for them.

Any people depicted in stock imagery provided by Getty Images are models,
and such images are being used for illustrative purposes only.
Certain stock imagery © Getty Images.

ISBN: 978-1-9736-8360-5 (sc)
ISBN: 978-1-9736-8359-9 (e)

Library of Congress Control Number: 2020900608

Print information available on the last page.

WestBow Press rev. date: 02/05/2020

DEDICATION

These devotionals are dedicated to you, my readers who encouraged me to combine them into a book. May you be challenged to love God more.

Helen McCormack

CONTENTS

Preface xiii

Acknowledgement xv

THE EARLY YEARS

Love and Old Ted 1

Of What is Your Memory Yarn Made? 4

Going to See Grandma 6

Are You Driven by Obsessions for Possessions? 9

What Kinds of Secrets Are We to Keep? 11

A Treasured Heritage or a Dust Collector? 13

Changed into Something New 15

Give Each Christmas an Eternal Perspective 17

Is it Good to be a Lone Ranger? 19

What Does the Future Hold? 22

Lessons in Prayer... 24

BECOMING

Confessions of Powers, Principalities and Particle Board.... 29

The Great Dill Pickle Debacle 32

Preparing for Christmas 34
Physical Pain and Spiritual Guilt.................................... 37
Discounting Rules Could Cost Us Our Lives................. 39
Treasures- Earthly or Heavenly? 42
No Pain No Gain.. 44
Trusting the Hand That Leads Us................................. 46
Learning from the Past and Planning for the Future 49
Pay Attention; Listen for Understanding 52
Who Is in Charge? 55

LITHUANIA

What Would Happen if We Seriously Sought God? 59
The One Who Trusts God is Invincible Part I 62
The One Who Trusts God is Invincible Part II 65
The Price of Freedom 68
Finding My Way in the Fog 70
Plenty and Want 72
Stuffing a Pillow Through a Funnel................................74

GERMANY

Treasuring God's Word 79
Outward Appearance or Internal Condition.................. 82
Pride and Humility 84
Have you Checked for Parasites Recently? 87
Understanding the Bible.. 90
Using our Spiritual Tools Correctly.............................. 92
Taking Freedom for Granted... 95
Don't Give the Enemy an Advantage............................. 97

Surprises in Life 100
We Might Fall When We Least Expect It.....................102
When the Leaning Post Moves....................................105
God Performs Miracles Today.....................................107
How Valuable Is Our Integrity?...................................110
God Still Performs Miracles 113

HOME AGAIN

The More We Own, the More We Are Owned............. 119
Tripping Hazards 122
Being Anchored to a Firm Foundation 124
Truth and God; Is There Really Only One Way?......... 126
Be Ready for the Lure of Temptation 128
Patience...131
Forgiven Is a Wonderful Place to Be.............................133
What We've Inherited 135
"Be still and Know that I am God" 137
What Would you Put in Your Obituary?.......................139

PREFACE

In many ways, my life has been ordinary. I grew up on a small dairy farm in Minnesota, went to grade school and high school and then college. I got a job, became engaged and then married. We had two children. My husband and I taught in various North Dakota towns for many years and later became missionaries serving in Lithuania and Germany.

Brilliantly interspersed in my ordinary life were touches from my extraordinary God: lessons He wanted to teach and insights He wanted me to understand about who He is. Some of my experiences are so ordinary that they could have been missed, some are humorous which shows God's sense of humor, some are sad because that's life sometimes and some are absolutely miraculous because He is the God of miracles.

My life has been pretty ordinary, but my God is extraordinary. I pray that you will be encouraged to seek Him more as you consider the lessons in these devotionals.

Acknowledgement

The devotionals in this book were developed because God prompted me to seek a venue for writing them. Thank you, Loretta Johnson (Religion Editor of the Minot Daily News in Minot, ND for many years) for believing in me enough to let me embark on the adventure of submitting them. Thank you, readers of the Reflections devotionals for encouraging me to compile them into a book. This book contains about one third of the devotionals that I've written over the last 20 plus years. Thank you to Bonnie Ler for reading and offering editing suggestions. Thank you Janese Lehman for editing and marketing assistance. Finally, but most importantly, thank you to my dear husband David of nearly 50 years for your wise suggestions, careful editing and loving encouragement so that this book might become a reality.

THE EARLY YEARS

LOVE AND OLD TED

After my grandparents purchased a Minnesota farm in 1914, they went in search of a dog. Hearing that a neighbor had one, my grandmother Erika loaded chickens into her wagon and headed down the road to work out a trade. Erika and her husband Abram soon discovered that "Old Ted" was a valuable, loving asset to the farm. Old Ted taught us a lot about Jesus.

For example, he frequently chased skunks off the farm and came home smelling like it. In later life, his eyesight suffered because of the frequency with which his eyes were sprayed. His sacrifice protected the family. In comparison, our God paid the ultimate sacrifice. He gave up his only Son so that Jesus would die to pay a debt we couldn't pay. "For God so loved the world that he gave his one and only Son, that whoever believes in him shall not perish but have eternal life." (John 3:16 NIV).

In another situation Abram went to investigate something he saw in the tall prairie grasses. The family continued working in the yard until Old Ted took off onto the prairie. No one had heard anything except Old Ted who found a bull threatening Abram. Old Ted chased that bull about a quarter mile through two fences before he was satisfied that Abram and everyone else on the farm was safe. God is an even stronger and more faithful protector. "...the Lord is faithful, and he will strengthen you and protect you from the evil one." (2 Thessalonians 3:3 NIV).

A particularly intriguing story was told by those who came to the farm when no one was home. If someone came onto the yard, Old Ted did nothing. If someone knocked on the door, Old Ted did nothing. However, if the visitor put his hand on the doorknob, Old Ted in turn put his mouth around the ankle of the visitor. I can't tell you what happened if the visitor turned the door knob since no one ever admitted trying it! Just as Old Ted guarded the house from intruders and possible danger, we need to ask God to help us guard what enters our hearts. "Above all else, guard your heart, for everything you do flows from it." (Proverbs 4:23 NIV).

Finally, even though he was strong and brave, just in time for milking Old Ted could gently bring the cows home. Jesus will gently guide us when we ask. "Take my yoke upon you and learn from me, for I am gentle and humble in heart, and you will find rest for your souls." (Matthew 11:29 NIV).

Old Ted was purchased with chickens. However, God's forgiveness is a free gift. If we do try to buy forgiveness with money or good words or deeds we are saying that what Jesus did when He died for us was not enough. "For it is by grace you have been saved, through faith—and this is not from yourselves, it is the gift of God not by works, so that no one can boast." (Ephesians 2:8-9 NIV).

Old Ted was an excellent example of a dog that had amazing talents to save, protect and guard. God is the perfect One who saves, protects, guards, loves, delights and sings over his children with joy. "The LORD your God is with you, the Mighty Warrior who saves. He will take great delight in you; in his love he will no longer rebuke you, but will rejoice over you with singing." (Zephaniah 3:17 NIV).

OF WHAT IS YOUR
MEMORY YARN MADE?

When I was a very little girl I often sat by the warm wood range in the kitchen while my mom washed dishes. Sometimes she taught me songs. I would then sing those songs from memory in church or school. In my earliest years, I would stand on a stool so that people could see me. I still love to sing but I almost never do it from memory anymore. I'm too afraid I'll forget the words and embarrass myself!

As I thought about all the songs I've memorized, I thought of Bible memorization. I confess that I don't spend much time committing scripture to memory. Is that true for you too? I suppose some of my excuses might sound like this: "I have lots of reference books handy; I can just look things up," or "Memorizing is such hard work," or even "I'm just too old to memorize anymore." If we are honest, I think we could all say that we CAN memorize.

But why should we bother memorizing scripture? An important reason for memorizing scripture is, "I have hidden your word in my heart that I might not sin against you." (Psalm 119:11 NIV). That is an amazing promise!

Apparently the verses I memorize become valuable tools that God will bring to mind when I am tempted.

Jesus quoted scripture when he was tempted by Satan. Jesus didn't need reference books but could quote the perfect verses that were already in His heart.

Often, that which is worthwhile takes effort. "My son, if you accept my words and store up my commands within you, turning your ear to wisdom and applying your heart to understanding, and if you call out for insight and cry aloud for understanding, and if you look for it as for silver and search for it as for hidden treasure, then you will understand the fear of the LORD and find the knowledge of God." (Proverbs 2:1-5 NIV). Look back over all the verbs in this passage. Earnest work is very beneficial as we study and apply the truths of the Bible, but don't miss the wonderful promise that follows!

Take some time this week to consider some verses you could learn. Ask God for his suggestions. For example, Psalm 139 is one I was challenged to learn with someone years ago and it is amazing how many times those verses come to mind in the way of challenge and/or comfort.

Write some verses on a piece of paper or card and put them on the mirror in the bathroom, at the kitchen sink, by your sewing machine, next to the chair where you rock your babies, next to the tools in your shop or on the TV screen! We can fill our hearts with many things; the cares of the day, the news of the world or the information from the gossip mill, but God's Word is of earthly encouragement and, even more importantly, of eternal value.

Going to See Grandma

"I'm going to see Grandma H tonight." I said, as my mother tucked me into bed.

I was six years old and had lived in bed for several months because of rheumatic fever which resulted in severe heart involvement. I was pale, thin and weak. I had been in and out of hospitals several times as doctors tried to find medicine that would help me.

My earlier childhood had been idyllic. I enjoyed playing on our small farm near a lake in Minnesota. I loved the smell and sparkle of that lake and listening to the waves lick the shoreline. I loved to listen to the birds and walk in the woods. Apple trees dotted the yard. There were two gardens that produced crisp carrots, tangy onions and sweet strawberries. I loved playing in my playhouse and creating mud pies that would have rivaled Sarah Lee's childhood pies.

During these days, however, life was different. My bed was placed in the living room to be near my parent's bedroom. There I played with my dolls and learned to read. If I had to go anywhere I was carried because I was too weak to walk.

Once, when I was having a very good day, my parents

entertained company. Since I was very flexible, I had impressed our guests by putting both feet behind my neck--at the same time. Later when I told my mother that I was going to see Grandma H, she became alarmed because that grandmother died when I was two.

I fell asleep but my mom checked on me several times until late in the night when she pulled my thumb from my mouth and in the light of the flashlight, saw that my thumb was tinged with blood. Not seeing a bite mark and realizing how lethargic I was, she knew that I was very ill. She called the doctor who came to our farm and drove us back to the hospital. Yes, I'm old enough for that to have happened! During that 8 mile drive from our farm to town, I remember commenting on the beauty of the stars. I was quickly told to lie very still and not talk. At the hospital the diagnosis indicated that I was experiencing pulmonary edema as a result of heart failure. If my mother had not recognized how ill I was, the doctor said I might not have lived more than one or two hours longer. "All the days ordained for me were written in Your book before one of them came to be." (Psalm 139:16b NIV). God was in control of that evening and prompted my mother to check on me. God knew that the days He had ordained for me had not yet ended. If it had been His will that I die that night, I would have. Nothing on earth could have prevented it.

Even though I didn't realize it, God had begun to teach me that I am not in control of life. I've needed several refresher courses on that topic since I have always struggled when I'm not in control. We don't know God's plans but we do know Who brought us into being and

Who ordered our days. That is enough. Some might view my life's beginning as a mistake, since I was born in 1946 to an unwed mother. However, I'm thankful that, with God, there are no mistakes in His plans for purpose or length of life.

Are You Driven by Obsessions for Possessions?

I was in elementary school when neck scarves became popular but I didn't have one. Every day I imagined the joy of having a scarf and the despair of never having one. I pictured how I would look in it. I imagined everyone admiring me. My desire ballooned as I fed it with my dreams. Eventually, it became my mother's nightmare!

One day I went to my mother and poured all my theatrics into the mournful tale that I didn't have a neck scarf like everyone else. At first my mother calmly reminded me that my birthday was only two days away and Christmas just three days after that so perhaps I would receive one. However, I refused to relent and I became more and more demanding. I cried and begged and became unbearable until my mother scolded me for my greed. Self pity completely enveloped me and I ran to my room crying.

Now, wishing to have a scarf was not necessarily wrong. But my obsession and resulting choice of behavior became sin for me.

As you might have already guessed, later that day a car drove into our farm yard bringing a school friend bearing a birthday present for me. She asked me to open it while she was there. Inside that box was a grey neck scarf with black telephones. (I remember it well!). I was deliriously happy. However, I also remember a nagging embarrassment because of my earlier behavior. Somehow, even as a child, I realized that my greed took some of the joy out of this coveted possession. Jesus said, "Watch out! Be on your guard against all kinds of greed; a man's life does not consist in an abundance of possessions." (Luke 12:15 NIV).

When Christmas or other events come, let's set aside obsessions for personal possessions and develop a broader focus with some of our gift giving. We could share this perspective with family and friends by giving some unique gifts. Organizations such as World Vision and Compassion International provide opportunities for this kind of giving to the needy of the world. Locally we might give to and assist The Salvation Army as well as many other worthy organizations.

Give a family in a third world country a goat so children have milk or a fishing kit so that a man can have the satisfaction of providing for his family. Fill a school pack for a needy child or give the joy of mobility for a child by purchasing a wheelchair. Perhaps there are those on our streets who could use the encouragement of a food basket, a warm coat, or a shoveled walk. The opportunities are endless and the cost varies. This kind of giving could last year round.

We should all rethink our approach as we consider gift giving or receiving. Let's honor God through all of our giving. Scripture tells us: "Truly, I say to you, as you did it to one of the least of these my brothers, you did to me." (Matthew 25:40 ESV).

WHAT KINDS OF SECRETS
ARE WE TO KEEP?

There are secrets we should have and secrets we shouldn't have.

When I was a little girl, my Mom and brother and I went shopping for my Dad's birthday present. I was given strict orders to keep the gift a secret. However, when we got home, I marched directly from the car to where Dad was working and said, "Guess what we got you for your birthday?" I then proceeded to tell him everything. I wasn't very good at keeping secrets!

At one time my husband and some friends planned a wonderful surprise party for one of my milestone birthdays. That was a great secret that many people kept!

However, there are secrets we shouldn't have. These secrets generally result from doing things we know we shouldn't. Could some of them sound like this?

"How much can I get away with?" asked the high school senior. "It's graduation night so I can't get suspended or expelled! I just won't tell the folks."

"No one will ever know," thinks the waitress, as she slips tip money that is supposed to go into the common pot, into her own pocket.

"Fireworks are against the law in town, but everybody does it. The police are too busy with other things on July 4th to care about a few fireworks in our back yard."

"The chances of an audit are so slim that I'm going to adjust the numbers on my return. I'll probably give more to the church. No one will ever know."

"We're almost out of paper for the printer at home and I don't want to go to the store. I'll just take a package from work. No one will miss it."

"I could take that purse this one time and then never steal again. When the store does inventory no one will know who took it."

How often do we try to justify something we know is wrong because we think that no one is watching? Actually, we never really have a secret since everything is known in the present. "You have set our iniquities before you, our secret sins in the light of your presence." (Psalm 90:8 ESV). "'Who can hide in secret places so that I cannot see them?' declares the LORD. "Do not I fill heaven and earth?" declares the LORD.'" (Jeremiah 23:24 NIV).

Our secrets will also be known in the future. Paul warned that the final judgment "will take place on the day when God will judge people's secrets through Jesus Christ, as my gospel declares." (Romans 2:16 NIV).

What kind of secrets are in our hearts? Are they things like birthdays, presents, parties and awards? That's great! Are they things like lust, lies, gossip and theft? Confess the sinful secrets to God and He will forgive. The ability to keep a secret isn't the criteria for making a decision to do or not do something. Truth and honesty are. We should desire to do only that which does not require us to keep a secret… except birthday surprises of course!

A Treasured Heritage
or a Dust Collector?

Each fall in north central North Dakota, the community gathers around Scandinavian specialties such as lutefisk, lefse, fattigmann, potato klub, and rosemaling. I enjoyed some of these traditions while growing up. My father loved lutefisk (cod cured with lye), especially when his mother served it with a spiced cream sauce. Almost everyone liked lefse (a potato based tortilla). My aunt made fattigmann (a light buttery pastry) at Christmas time. Whatever your cultural heritage, there are probably similar traditions that have been passed on from generation to generation.

There are many types of traditions passed on through families. Some may be positive and some may be negative. One positive tradition passed on in my family was Bible reading. Every evening, before bed my brother and I gathered around the dining room table with our parents to read a chapter from the Bible. This continued after my brother and I left home. After my father's death in 1990 my mother told me that they were on the 14th reading of the entire Bible. She continued the tradition until her own death in 2015.

When I was a child I remember waiting eagerly to be old enough to begin taking my turn reading the Bible out loud. I would haltingly read two or three verses and then my father would finish the chapter. Almost nothing interfered with this practice. If someone was sick with the flu, the family would gather around their bed and the reading would go on as usual. I value that heritage. I learned Bible stories when I was young and had daily exposure to the importance of God's truths that could apply to daily life.

Unfortunately, this tradition does not exist in many homes today. Even sadder is the fact that there are children in my local city who do not know what a Bible is, much less what it teaches. God's truth is not valued as God instructed us to value it when he said, "Fix these words of mine in your hearts and minds; tie them as symbols on your hands and bind them on your foreheads. Teach them to your children, talking about them when you sit at home and when you walk along the road, when you lie down and when you get up. Write them on the doorframes of your houses and on your gates…" (Deuteronomy 11:18-20a NIV). Culturally, the scriptures were to be part of everyday activities and even physical attire as a reminder to serve God faithfully. David describes another way to use scripture when he writes, "I have hidden your word in my heart that I might not sin against you." (Psalm 119:11 NIV). God's word cannot be hidden in our hearts if we do not know it.

In our homes, is the Bible and the truths it teaches part of a treasured heritage or is the Bible just a dust collector?

CHANGED INTO SOMETHING NEW

"Helen has a serious throat infection and must go to the hospital," the doctor said to my mother.

While I was in the hospital, my schoolteacher gave me a book called "The Triplets Receive a Reward" (published by Eerdmans 1946). It was a story about fifth graders like me; Iona, Iva and Ted Behr and the trouble maker Andy. He teased everyone but especially enjoyed calling Ted a "cute Teddy Bear." Worse yet, he worked hard to get Ted in trouble. In spite of this, Ted and his sisters always tried to be kind. This frustrated Andy and he asked Ted why he was so nice to him. Ted told him that it was because when he became a Christian, God changed him.

One day Iona and Andy had a long visit about what it means to be a Christian. She told him that a Christian is one who has asked Jesus to forgive his sins and ask Jesus to take over his life. Andy didn't have a Bible so Iona gave him one and pointed out "For God so loved the world that He gave his only Son, that whoever believes in Him should not perish but have eternal life." (John 3:16 ESV).

Andy started reading the Bible, and after asking Iona

many more questions, he decided to ask God to forgive him. After that Andy's behavior began to change.

I was fascinated, and read about becoming a Christian over and over. I had always tried to be nice and I had gone to church as long as I could remember, but this was different. I decided that I wanted to become a Christian too.

Hospital rules during the 1950's were very strict, especially for children! When the nurses turned the lights out at night, turning them on again was strictly forbidden! So alone, after the lights were out in the hospital, I quietly slid the book and a flashlight under the covers and read again how to ask Jesus to forgive my sin. I followed their example in prayer and meant it sincerely. God gave me the gift to understand that I was forgiven and that God was now a part of my life. Since Andy had been told to read the Bible and pray every day I decided I needed to do that too.

After getting well, I went back to school. There was a small lake across the road from my one-room schoolhouse and we were trying to learn to skate that winter. I was a poor skater and after falling for the "tenth" time, I decided that I must look pretty silly and laughed till my sides hurt. To my surprise, on our way back to the school at the end of recess, one friend said, "You know, you've been different since you came back from the hospital; a good different." I was amazed. Even though I had never been as mean as Andy, the Lord was apparently changing me into a new person too.

Are you longing for a change? Have you asked God to forgive your sins? You too can follow God's call and He will become an intimate part of your life, changing you. He promises: "Therefore, if anyone is in Christ he is a new creation, the old has gone, the new has come." (2 Corinthians 5:17 NIV).

GIVE EACH CHRISTMAS AN ETERNAL PERSPECTIVE

―――――――――

As I look back into my childhood, I remember our annual church's Christmas program with sweet memories. Shopping for a new dress, practicing and remembering the birthday of Jesus filled me with excitement. After the program there was a bag of candy, nuts and the sweetest, juiciest apple of the year.

Everything about those Christmases was wonderful except for one thing. When people talked about Jesus coming to earth as a baby to later die for our sins they proceeded to talk about Jesus returning to earth again. That idea gave me a sick feeling in the pit of my stomach. I was actually scared silly. I wanted life to continue on earth as I knew it. I didn't want eternity to begin. However, after I asked Jesus into my life I no longer feared Jesus because I knew that he didn't come to condemn me but saw me as forgiven because I accepted Jesus' sacrifice for me.

As I've "matured" even more, I look at eternity with a whole new perspective. I'm also prompted to think about a question I once heard. Are we living for the dot or the line?

The line is eternity. God had no beginning and He has

no end. It is really hard to wrap our brains around a concept like that. Compared to eternity, the approximately 80 years most live on this earth is just a dot.

Living for the dot means that our energies are spent on obtaining and maintaining as many possessions as possible. However, when it comes down to it, we can't have everything; so we are never satisfied. Besides, if we had everything where would we put it?

Living for the line means that our earthly focus is on the eternal God. God's perspective drives our motives and priorities since, as a friend once said, the more we own, the more we are owned. Earthly possessions with an eternal perspective are explained in Jesus' instruction when he says, "Do not store up for yourselves treasures on earth, where moth and rust destroy, and where thieves break in and steal. Store up for yourselves treasures in heaven, where moth and rust do not destroy and where thieves do not break in and steal." (Matthew 6:19-20 NIV).

Everyone will have an eternity. In Matthew 25, Jesus speaks of the eternity of all mankind. He says that for those who do not accept salvation on His terms, there is eternal hell. For those who do accept salvation on His terms, there is eternal heaven.

Thoughts of eternity may sound scary, boring or silly to those who live only for the dot. I pray that we will all grow to have God's eternal perspective about earthly life. This can be done by reading the Bible, seeking out a church that teaches the Bible clearly and ultimately accepting God's perspective in everyday life.

Let's consider our lives in the light of this question. Are we living for the dot or the line?

IS IT GOOD TO BE A LONE RANGER?

During my first 8 years of education, I attended a one room school with a population that ranged from 16 students to eventually only 4 students. I loved the familiarity as each school year started. However, when I headed into a larger school for grade 9, where there were 129 in my grade alone, I struggled to find my way in the comparatively massive building. Gradually, my comfort level grew except at the end of the day. When my last class ended I would leave the classroom, go up the stairs, across a hall, down the stairs, around the corner and down the hall to my locker. Every day I puzzled at how others who had been in the same class and had lockers near mine, were gone or almost ready to leave every time I arrived at my locker. I stepped up the pace day after day, nearly running my route, but I was always later than everyone else.

One day as I walked around a corner I'd not visited before I stopped in shock. There was my 7th hour classroom and my locker was just behind me!! No wonder everyone else beat me to the lockers! My stress, frustration and embarrassment, then and now, were wasted energy because

I was too shy and independent to ask for help. Obviously there was no blood and no one died but it must have been traumatic or I wouldn't still remember it.

A similar independent attitude and mind set was evident in a child who cried for three days before kindergarten started because that child had not yet learned to read! No amount of reasoning assured the child that the work in school would be age appropriate. Only when the mom and child walked into kindergarten the first day of school and the child looked at the coloring paper on the desk, did a glimmer of hope appear as the child said, "I can do this!" Even though the child's perception of kindergarten was unrealistic, at least this child talked about fears and frustrations while I bottled mine up inside, trying harder to prove that I could do things on my own.

I believe that many people approach their Christian lives similarly. Either they struggle on alone or they become overwhelmed by their unreasonable worries so they live in constant anxiety, worry and needy control. I know I have done both. Should we tell our struggles to everyone? No, we shouldn't open our second floor windows and yell our sins to the four winds. However, we should find a trusted friend to pray for and with us when we are heavy laden with life's burdens and challenges. We can do the same for them!

The Bible is very direct in its admonition that we not live our Christian lives as Lone Rangers. "We urge you, brothers and sisters, warn those who are idle and disruptive, encourage the disheartened, help the weak, be patient with everyone." (1 Thessalonians 5:14 NIV). "…Strive for full restoration, encourage one another, be of one mind, live in peace…" (2 Corinthians 13:11 NIV). "Therefore encourage one another and build each other up…" (1 Thessalonians 5:11 NIV). "… Preach the word; be prepared in season and out of season; correct, rebuke and encourage—with great patience and careful instruction." (2 Timothy 4:2 NIV).

Christianity is not about walking into a church on Sunday morning. It's about relationship; first between Jesus and us and then between Jesus, us and other Christians. Find, and be, an encourager instead of struggling alone.

WHAT DOES THE
FUTURE HOLD?

It was pretty exciting when we got our first telephones! We could contact our neighbors by turning a phone crank to ring a long and a short or two shorts. If someone had told me that someday I could carry a phone in my purse that could reach around the world with the touch of my finger, I would have been doubtful. As a child, communication with anyone far away was in the form of a letter with a three cent stamp!

If someone had told me as a child that someday we would have computers that could send messages across the world in seconds, I would not have believed it. The future has a way of surprising us by its unbelievable developments!

What does the Bible say about our eternal future?

One promise is that Jesus will return. "So you also must be ready, because the son of man will come at an hour when you do not expect him." (Matthew 24:44 NIV). We are given examples of when people were told to be ready for God's plan to unfold but were still caught by surprise. "As it was in the days of Noah, so it will be at the coming of the Son of Man. For in the days before the flood, people were eating and drinking, marrying and giving in marriage, up to the day Noah entered the ark…" (Matthew 24:37-38 NIV). "It was the same in the days of Lot. People were eating and drinking, buying and selling, planting and building. But the day Lot left Sodom, fire and sulfur rained down from heaven and destroyed them all. It will be just like this on the day the Son of Man is revealed." (Luke 17:28-30 NIV).

All will see the return of Jesus even if they don't believe it is probable. "Then will appear the sign of the Son of Man in heaven. And then all peoples of the earth will mourn when they see the Son of Man coming on the clouds of heaven, with power and great glory." (Matthew 24: 30 NIV).

Does a feeling of doom build in our hearts when we think about these things? It used to for me! However, after knowing God more, I feel differently. I don't mean that knowing more facts about God has given me peace even though that helps us understand His character. I have peace for the future because there is a personal relationship and growing trust in who God is. With this relationship, I'm going to spend eternity with a friend, not a stranger. Besides, Jesus promised those who have a relationship with him that he has a plan, "Do not let your hearts be troubled. You believe in God, believe also in me. My Father's house has many rooms; if that were not so, would I have told you that I am going there to prepare a place for you?" (John 14:1-3 NIV). With all the evidence that Biblical prophecies do come true, the facts above give us a glimpse of a future that anyone who has a relationship with Jesus can get excited about!

LESSONS IN PRAYER

During college years I was involved as a leader with a campus Christian organization. Mr. Olson, our faculty advisor, had been very helpful as we began our year. We would sometimes go to his office or even his home to discuss general leadership details and our plans for the year. I remember very well, however, the first time we went to his home with a significant problem. He warmly invited us in and asked how we were. We poured out our dilemma and then asked, "What should we do?" He very calmly asked, "Have you prayed about it?" We honestly answered, "No." He then headed toward his door saying, "Then I certainly can't help you." Come back, if you need to...after you've prayed."

In a shocked state we started home. I admit that we were put out by his response. We couldn't believe that he would turn us away when we most needed his help. However, we begrudgingly decided we better do as he asked and we spent time praying about our situation. Are you surprised that our problem did work itself out?

Later we had an even more challenging problem and we wanted to ask Mr. Olson what to do but this time we prayed first. However, our problem remained unsolved. We decided to give Mr. Olson a try again so we went to his home and said that we needed his help. He asked the expected question, "Have you prayed about it?" This time we answered with a resounding "Yes." He then invited us to sit down and we spent time in his living room praying, discussing our problem and brainstorming possible solutions. He was a great help.

It was only later that I realized the full impact of what he was teaching us. Don't use prayer as a last resort, but as the first offense in all of life as taught in the Bible.

Jesus taught by example: "After he had dismissed them, he went up on a mountainside by himself to pray." (Matthew 14:23 NIV).

Jesus gave a reason for prayer: "Watch and pray so that you will not fall into temptation. The spirit is willing, but the flesh is weak." (Matthew 26:41 NIV).

Individual prayer is not negotiable: "But when you pray, go into your room, close the door and pray to your Father, who is unseen." (Matthew 6:6a NIV).

Corporate prayer was modeled in the early church: "When they arrived, they went upstairs to the room where they were staying. Those present were Peter, John, James and Andrew; Philip and Thomas, Bartholomew and Matthew; James son of Alphaeus and Simon the Zealot, and Judas son of James. They all joined together constantly in prayer, along with the women and Mary the mother of Jesus, and with his brothers." (Acts 1:13-14 NIV).

There is a corporate prayer topic: "Therefore confess your sins to each other and pray for each other so that you may be healed." (James 5:16a NIV).

There is a role of prayer in difficult relationships: "But I tell you: Love your enemies and pray for those who persecute you." (Matthew 5:44 NIV).

There is to be a constant attitude of prayer: "Pray continually." (1 Thessalonians 5:17 NIV).

These references merely scratch the surface of God's desire that prayer become foundational to all of life, both individually and corporately. Then, prayer will take its proper place as the first offense when we face dilemmas.

BECOMING

CONFESSIONS OF POWERS, PRINCIPALITIES AND PARTICLE BOARD

"Helen Ann, come back here and close that door properly," my mother said as I stormed out of the house in one of my childhood tirades. In spite of my bent toward door slamming, I was basically compliant so I walked back up the steps, opened and closed the door quietly. My external behavior changed, but as we will see, the desire to give in to that behavior still existed.

As I grew up I slammed doors less and less, especially in the presence of my mother, but it was still a temptation. I remember being angry about something during the first few months of marriage. I don't know what it was about now but after my husband left to teach, I stormed through our 10' X 45' rented mobile home, doing dishes, folding laundry and preparing to teach in the afternoon. All the while, I took advantage of the opportunity to slam every door and drawer available.

After one especially hefty slam, I saw with horror that the front of a particle board drawer had fallen off and was lying at my feet. Panicked, I picked it up, determined to fix it so no one would know what I had done. With a sinking heart, I soon conceded that I had indeed broken the drawer beyond my ability to fix it. I had never intended to do this damage to rented property and I felt just terrible. I knew it had to be repaired and I knew my husband would know how to do it. However, that also meant that I would have to confess how it happened. I grew in humility that day!

I had learned to control some behavior, but the desire was still in my heart. I was a Christian, forgiven because Jesus died for me and because I accept that as my only way to heaven. However, my sin nature had not died and won't die until I do.

Even the apostle Paul struggled with his inborn sin nature when he said, "For I have the desire to do what is good, but I cannot carry it out. For I do not do the good I want to do, but the evil I do not want to do-this I keep on doing." (Romans 7:18b-19 NIV). We will struggle with sin till the day we die. The Bible describes ongoing spiritual battles including the battle against sin. "For our struggle is not against flesh and blood, but against the rulers, against the authorities, against the powers of this dark world and against the spiritual forces of evil in the heavenly realms." (Ephesians 6:12 ESV). Acknowledging our basic sin nature is not an excuse to keep sinning, but it helps to realize that this struggle will continue. We need to pray and find accountable partners so that we can grow stronger.

So, what did my husband say when I confessed my bad behavior? He was very forgiving and quietly repaired the drawer so it looked and worked like new. He did not berate or shame me. God is even more like that. We can come to Him sincerely confessing our sin and He will quietly forgive.

Sometimes, however, we must accept that there may be natural consequences because of our sinful choices. When we confess our sin, He will take us in His arms and say, "Let him who is without sin among you be the first to throw a stone...." (John 8:7b RSV).

THE GREAT DILL PICKLE DEBACLE

I had been married a little over a year and we were living in a new community. When a funeral was announced at our church, I saw an opportunity to be of service and get to know some of the ladies. I arrived at the church early, headed to the kitchen and asked what I might do to help. They seemed surprised, but pleased. They decided to have me slice the dill pickles. As I began slicing, I realized that I was not good at making traditional dill wedges. They were thin on some ends and thick on others so I decided to cut them in flat slices similar to Stackers on the shelves today. They looked lovely even though I was 30 years ahead of my time! I sliced and sliced until I had the dishes filled for all the tables in the fellowship hall.

Just as I finished I was surprised by a gasp and loud exclamation, "What did you do with the pickles? We don't slice them that way! Oh my!"

Since all the jars were empty and all the dishes full, the ladies decided, after some noisy and stressful discussion, that they would have to serve them. I was very uncomfortable and didn't know what to say or what to do.

Just as the women started to set those "embarrassing" pickles on the tables, one of the younger ladies slipped passed me and whispered in my ear, "Don't let it bother you. We'll talk!" Our talk was very encouraging and she and I became very good friends.

"How ridiculous," you might be thinking, "all that fuss over a few pickles!" Is it ridiculous? Have you ever had heated discussions over trivial things? Is it the color of the carpet, the thickness of the pew cushion, the organization of the kitchen or the amount the pastor is paid? Since these things are of no eternal consequence shouldn't our energy be spent on more eternal things such as Bible reading, prayer, in-depth study and scripture application through our relationships as we encourage one another in our spiritual growth? Shouldn't we share our material possessions with those in need? Shouldn't we spend time planning out-reach to our local college students, providing spiritual training and healthy activities for our young people, caring for the needs of the elderly, and giving love and attention to those with special needs? We should "Fix our eyes not on what is seen, but on what is unseen since what is seen is temporary, but what is unseen is eternal." (2 Corinthians 4:18 NIV).

When we get to heaven, I doubt that the Lord will commend our preference for green carpet over blue. Rather, He will ask, "Did you feed my sheep?" (John 21:17 ESV).

PREPARING FOR CHRISTMAS

At the coming of our daughter in 1979, my mother in law began a project of love. She obtained some fabric and embroidered (and she was excellent!) pictures of babies on each of 9 large fabric blocks. When finished, she sewed the blocks together. Then life happened and the intended quilt was never completed. Now our daughter is married and has children of her own. After her daughter was born, I remembered that quilt top that was stored in a cedar chest and decided it would be the perfect Christmas gift. We found backing and border fabric, added batting and sewed it together finishing it with baby yarn. Two generations of love and 36 years later the quilt was finished.

That gift took a long time to finish but how about a gift that could be traced back 42 generations (at least 1,000 years) as laid out in the first chapter of Matthew? We might be tempted to skip the names but they give historical credibility to the lineage of Jesus. In Psalm 89:3-4, for example, we read that Jesus would come from the lineage of David and David's name is included in the Matthew list.

In addition to Jesus' lineage, there are hints of the gift of Jesus sprinkled throughout the Old Testament. There are at least 68 references to the life of Jesus in the book of Psalms alone. Even as early as Genesis 3, God challenges the deceiving serpent as he speaks about Jesus' death and resurrection. In Psalm 22:16 we read that Jesus would be pierced. That piercing is described in the Gospel accounts of Jesus' death. See especially Matthew 27:38.

In Isaiah we read of Jesus birth to a virgin. "Therefore, the Lord Himself will give you a sign: The virgin will be with a child and will give birth to a son, and will call him Immanuel." (Isaiah 7:14 NIV). The Gospels confirm that Jesus was born of a virgin.

When the Wise Men came to find Jesus, King Herod, fearing some other king would take his place, asked his scholars where this Christ was to be born. They found the answer in scripture. "But you, Bethlehem, in the land of Judah, are by no means least among the rulers of Judah; for out of you will come a ruler who will be the shepherd of my people Israel." (Micah 5:2 NIV).

Since Jesus was found in Bethlehem, King Herod, wanting to be sure that this "would be" king would be stopped, had all the boys 2 years and younger killed. That mass murder was prophesied. "A voice is heard in Ramah, mourning and great weeping, Rachel weeping for her children and refusing to be comforted, because her children are no more." (Jeremiah 31:15 NIV).

There is even mention that Jesus would teach in parables in Psalm 78:2. By reading in Matthew 13 as well as many other passages, we know that this was true.

These and many other Bible passages reveal God's plan of a special gift for us. Jesus' birth, life, death and resurrection are the gift that gives eternal life in heaven to all who will accept it. That is what we celebrate every Christmas. Actually, we can celebrate that gift every day!

PHYSICAL PAIN AND
SPIRITUAL GUILT

Someone once said to me, "I don't like Christianity because it's a religion based on guilt." While the complete truth of that statement may be debatable, an understanding of the purpose of guilt is important. Perhaps the following will help.

Several years ago I woke up one day feeling ill and with a nagging pain in my right side. I was teaching part time and this Monday I was off. I slowly did laundry and cleaned house. On Tuesday I felt fine and did my teaching. Wednesday the pain was back and was even more persistent. I mentioned it to other teachers during a break. One had experienced this kind of pain two months before and said I should go to the emergency room because it sounded like it could be my appendix.

I worked in a small town and the doctor came only certain days for a few hours. He was there that afternoon so I went to the emergency room where they drew blood and did some prodding of my abdomen. Yes, indeed! They found the spot! By 10:00 that evening, I was recovering from an appendectomy.

In the same way that the pain of my appendix drove

me to seek a doctor, the guilt (symptom) we feel for our sin should drive us to God as we admit the truth of our action and condition. The Ten Commandments given in the Old Testament, and confirmed in the New Testament, provide a standard under which we are to live. We haven't obeyed these laws perfectly so we experience guilt which makes us aware of our need. Admitting our need for God and confessing our sin to him can feel like personal trauma. However, after the confession we have peace because, just as my appendix is gone forever, confessed sins are gone forever. God promised: "For I will forgive their wickedness and will remember their sins no more." (Hebrews 8:12 NIV).

Jesus' purpose in coming to earth was to heal guilty people. Jesus was reprimanded by religious leaders for associating with people thought to be too evil to be around. On hearing this, "Jesus said to them, It is not the healthy who need a doctor, but the sick. I have not come to call the righteous, but sinners." (Mark 2:17 NIV).

I've established an ongoing relationship with my doctor so that as other things go wrong with my body, we can deal with them. We need to maintain a similar relationship with God since as humans, we can never be perfect. Therefore, present sins, which bring guilt, can also be forgiven.

The pain of the appendix was a gift because it may have saved my physical life. Guilt is also a gift because it brings us to God for forgiveness which saves our souls eternally.

"May the God of hope fill you with all joy and peace as you trust in him, so that you may overflow with hope by the power of the Holy Spirit." (Romans 15:13 NIV).

DISCOUNTING RULES COULD COST US OUR LIVES.

In 1973 I was tutoring a homebound child. Because of bad weather I hadn't gone to their farm for several days so in spite of -30°F temperatures with a 40 mph wind, I decided I had to go.

The first of many snow drifts I encountered was huge and after I arrived at the farm we agreed that I should have stayed home. I quickly gathered completed papers, gave assignments and left.

As I approached that huge drift again I was amazed that my earlier tracks were gone and the drift was even larger. I was usually timid in the face of large drifts but I knew this demanded courage. So I took off aggressively into the drift. However, as the deep snow pulled me back and forth my confidence turned to fear which turned to panic and I slammed on the breaks. Do you know what happens when you do that in the middle of a huge drift? Nothing good!! I made a 90 degree turn into the ditch! I could only get the passenger's door open so I considered the rules.

First, never leave your car. I rationalized that it would be hours before the busses came, if they came at all! Town never disappeared in spite of the storm so I believed I wouldn't get lost. I knew it was cold but I had lots of clothes and it wasn't far.

However, after one minute down the road, I felt naked. Another five minutes and my legs started getting stiff. Weariness and fear threatened to overtake me but I finally got to town and found help. As I directed the tow truck to my car the drivers exclaimed, "You walked half a mile in this weather!?!" I realized that I had discounted lots of rules that could have cost me my life.

There are many who discount God's rules too. I've heard some say that they don't believe we're sinners. But God's rules say, "For all have sinned and fall short of the glory of God." (Romans 3:23 NIV).

I've heard some say that there are many ways to heaven. God's rules say that "Salvation is found in no one else, for there is no other name (but Jesus) under heaven given to mankind by which we must be saved." (Acts 4:12 NIV). Some discount, "no other name" and try to get to heaven by doing what they think will work rather than what God's rules say.

I've heard some say that a God of both love and justice is incompatible. God's love for us nailed Jesus to the cross. God's judgment on us because we've broken His rules also nailed Jesus to the cross. Our sin requires justice, the death penalty. God's love let Jesus take that death penalty for us. We can't earn it. We must accept the rules Jesus established. "For it is by grace you have been saved, through faith—and this is not from yourselves, it is the gift of God…" (Ephesians 2:8 NIV). Discounting God's work will cost us our eternal lives in heaven.

By the way, the father of my student became concerned when I didn't answer my home phone and came looking for me, risking his own safety. Jesus gave up his very life to help us. Run to him and enjoy the peace of forgiveness, the joy of a secure eternity and the rest found only in God's loving arms. "The name of the Lord is a fortified tower; the righteous run to it and are safe." (Proverbs 18:10 NIV).

Treasures- Earthly or Heavenly?

One summer I drove through the area in Minnesota where I grew up. As I traveled down the road toward the farm my mind flowed back through many memories.

I saw the backdrop of a sparkling lake dotted with fishing boats in the summer or fish houses in the winter. I saw the two story white farm house, garage, red barn, two chicken houses, the pump house for cooling milk and a large red granary. Scattered between the buildings were apple trees and several lush gardens full of flowers, potatoes, vegetables, raspberries, strawberries and tomatoes. An irrepressible smile spread over me as I remembered a particular tree in the yard. It once served as a panic brake when I was learning to ride my bike! I also remembered my dad lying under that same tree on occasional warm Sunday afternoons. As a child I was puzzled that someone could waste time napping on a perfectly good afternoon.

My mind longed to linger and bask in more memories but I was brought back to the present as familiar land marks appeared. My anticipation mounted. I knew the farm had changed, but I longed to see glimpses of my memories.

As I topped the hill and scanned the scene I was dismayed

to see that huge lake homes had invaded everything. The only familiar landmarks were the once red granary and the remains of a garage.

As I drove away, a little sad that I couldn't see the friendly farm yard with my eyes once more, the Lord brought a verse to mind, "Heaven and earth will pass away, but my words will never pass away." (Matthew 24:35 NIV).

I pondered that verse as we drove two miles down the road to see the church I attended as a child. I knew that it too had been replaced with a new one. I was not drawn to the new building because there were no childhood memories there. I only paused at my father's grave and then drove away thinking again of the temporary nature of this earth compared to the permanence of God's kingdom.

We work hard to gain more and more earthly possessions, but all those things we gather will be only a memory some day. Actually, even the memories will eventually be gone. The people living on our farm yard know nothing of my memories. That doesn't really matter because we should not secure our physical or mental treasures to this earth. "Do not lay up for yourselves treasures on earth, where moths and rust destroy and where thieves break in and steal. But lay up for yourselves treasures in heaven, where neither moth nor rust destroys and where thieves do not break in and steal. For where your treasure is, there your heart will be also." (Matthew 6:19-20 ESV).

I'm learning to hold earthly "treasures" loosely but I am also working to grip more firmly to heaven's unchangeable treasures since "His dominion is an everlasting dominion that will not pass away, and his kingdom is one that will never be destroyed." (Daniel 7:14b NIV). What kinds of treasures are you holding with your heart and mind?

No Pain No Gain

Some years ago we remodeled an old house. We knocked plaster off walls in order to access plumbing because there were places where it leaked. We removed walls and put walls in different places in order to improve traffic flow. We accessed enough studs to run new wiring since the old was definitely not up to the required code. Sometimes we were tired and discouraged, but as rooms started to take shape we felt renewed energy. We knew that ultimately, in order to pass inspection, we had to do our work correctly.

In the same way, athletes run, stretch, lift weights and sweat in order to excel. If they want to gain in strength and ability, they must work hard and submit to a coach who helps them see their weaknesses and capitalize on their strengths. If they don't listen to instruction, they don't improve their skills. If they are team members and are willing to follow the rules, the whole team benefits.

In comparison, farmers spend long hours planning for each growing season. They repair equipment, purchase fertilizer and quality seed. They visit with other farmers and read about tilling methods, planting techniques and weed control. They sweat in the hot sun to harvest the crop. With a good crop, the family has food and greater income. As crops are then sold, many benefit.

Finally, store owners and business operators, plan their inventory according to the needs of their community. For example, no matter how much someone might love selling snow blowers, there probably isn't a market for them in Hawaii. So they order, advertise, prepare displays and do all they can to maintain the necessary items. This is done for the personal gain of the owner and/or the businesses.

These are just a few examples of the necessity of planning for success which is not likely to happen automatically but must be worked for. The same should be true of our Christian lives. If we are to grow as Christians, (sanctification) we must read the Bible, we must pray, and we must listen to instruction. We must evaluate ourselves as we seek to become more like God, not to earn His favor but to respond in thankfulness for the sacrifice of His son in payment for the punishment we deserve. We do this with the help of the Holy Spirit and for God's glory, not our own. We must listen to Biblical instruction and submit to Godly church leadership. Sometimes it's uncomfortable to admit our weaknesses. However, spiritual growth not only results in a richer life on earth, but an eternal life, full of worship and praise to our God. To grow spiritually we need regular encouragement and guidance. Those in our churches who teach and lead us spiritually are called to that task. "Obey your leaders and submit to them, for they are keeping watch over your souls, as those who will have to give an account. Let them do this with joy and not with groaning, for that would be of no advantage to you." (Hebrews 13:17 ESV).

TRUSTING THE HAND
THAT LEADS US

Recently we had the pleasure of visiting our 15 month old granddaughter…and her parents of course! I acted like any grandparent by concluding that she was the sweetest and smartest grandchild ever! If she wanted her father to pet her stuffed dog, she would take his hand and lay it on the head of the dog. If she wanted to go somewhere, even though she could walk alone, she would often find the hand of her mother or father and lead them toward the place she wanted to go. When she wanted help picking up her chair that had tipped, she came to me, took my hand and laid it on the chair. She had learned that the adults in her life can provide companionship by engaging in the same activity of petting her stuffed dog. She had learned that she can lead her parents to explore with her and provide her with encouragement and support. She had learned that adults can help make things right.

I believe that in the same way that she looked for a hand for companionship, encouragement and help, we should take God's hand as we walk through life. We can seek God for companionship because He loves his children. "See what great love the Father has lavished on us, that we should be called children of God." (1 John 3:1 NIV). We can seek God for encouragement because he will always listen and respond to our needs. "You, Lord, hear the desire of the afflicted; you encourage them, and you listen to their cry." (Psalm 10:17 NIV). God can also give us help during the challenges of life. God did this for David in a practical way as David sought to understand how God wanted his temple built. "All this," David said, "I have in writing as a result of the Lord's hand on me, and he enabled me to understand all the details of the plan." (1 Chronicles 28:19 NIV).

Sometimes, especially when our granddaughter wanted to go places unsafe or touch things that could hurt her, her parents would try to redirect her or remove her from harm. She didn't always appreciate her parents' decisions. We naturally understand that a 15 month old doesn't have enough experience to understand the potential dangers in her world. However, when God redirects us or tries to distract us from something He knows is harmful we adults sometimes act like we have greater knowledge and understanding than God. We fight, complain and whine when we are not allowed to do something we think we want or when we are made to do something against our preferences. This makes life even harder. When Saul (later Paul) met God for the first time, God said to Saul. "Saul, Saul, why do you persecute me? It is hard for you to kick against the goads." (Acts 26:14b NIV). During Bible times, a goad was a long stick with a pointed piece of iron at the end. It was used to direct oxen to go where they were supposed to go. However, if the oxen kicked back against the goad they would receive much more prick than was intended. God's point was that Saul had been making life harder for himself by fighting against God. We need to take God's hand and trust him in the good and bad times because he is trustworthy and knows best. "The works of his hands are faithful and just; all his precepts are trustworthy." (Psalm 111:7 NIV).

LEARNING FROM THE PAST AND PLANNING FOR THE FUTURE

Thoughts about our past can fill us with joy and/or regret. Thoughts about the future are often hopeful but sometimes laced with fear. Our attitudes about our past and future affect what we do in that fleeting moment we call the present. Let's consider a few examples.

Earlier this year I let someone's dog out. He likes to jump the fence so a long tether is attached to the inside doorknob. I hooked the tether to his collar, opened the door and he bounded out happily. As I watched him, something suddenly caught his visual attention and he bolted. I quickly learned that it is never a good idea to have your head between the door and the door frame when a large dog is tethered to that same door!

In a different vein, my spring fatigue prompted my doctor to send me to a cardiologist who placed a stent in a major artery that was 95% blocked. God was gracious in protecting me from a heart attack.

Similarly, my aunt passed away last summer at the age of 91 leaving my generation at the "top" age wise. I feel a responsibility to live in the present in a manner that points younger generations to understand that we have an eternal future and that there is more to life than earthly things.

When I was in grade school I looked forward to my future in high school. After that I looked forward to college and the possibility of enjoyable employment, marriage, children and grandchildren. I looked forward to special vacations and family gatherings. What's after that? It's old age and I would venture to guess that very few look forward to that because it often means losses. It means losing those close to us, having our activity restricted and needing help with the basics of life. It could mean the loss of mental abilities. Given these potential future realities, I've asked myself how I should view my remaining years be it 1 or 25. I've concluded that I need to view them as gifts in which God can still use me if I seek His wisdom, patience and grace so that I can respond to others with love, peace and a noncritical spirit. I need to learn from my past but live for the future. I do know that my own future in heaven is secure because Jesus paid the price I could not pay for my sin and I've received Him as my Savior. My ongoing prayer needs to be that of the Psalmist. "Teach us to number our days that we may gain a heart of wisdom." (Psalm 90:12 NIV).

We are given a glimpse of what the eternal future will be like for the Christian. "And I heard a loud voice from the throne saying, 'Look! God's dwelling place is now among the people, and he will dwell with them. They will be his people, and God himself will be with them and be their God. He will wipe every tear from their eyes. There will be no more death or mourning or crying or pain, for the old order of things has passed away.'" (Revelation 21:3-5 NIV).

Note that this does not refer to material possessions but to spiritual ones. Knowing this, I don't need to dread losses on this earth but I can live with purpose as I learn more and more about the God with whom I will spend my eternal future. I pray that is true for you as well.

PAY ATTENTION; LISTEN FOR UNDERSTANDING

It was a lovely day and I was asked to take two large, energetic dogs for a walk. I was hesitant because I knew these dogs were strong. I was assured, though, that we would do just fine if I held the leashes exactly as I was told.

The excited dogs were brought from the house, tails wagging fiercely, eyes bright with eager anticipation, bodies tense with expectation. I took the leashes and we headed off down the street at a very brisk pace. We had only gone a short distance when I knew that something was wrong. One dog was on my left and the other was on my right but each leash was wrapped behind my legs. If the dogs decided to take off after something, I was in big trouble. I paused to rethink the instructions I had been given. As I tried to detangle myself, two barking dachshunds "attacked." My charges rushed to meet them forcing me forward onto the pavement. The next thing I knew I was hanging on to the two leashes with all my might as I was dragged down the street. When would they notice that I was still there?

I was rescued by the dachshunds' owners who whisked them away. Once my dogs' point of interest was gone, they noticed that I was on the ground and they romped over to me with renewed excitement wondering if perhaps I wanted to play! Amidst a web of energetic bodies, wagging tails and kissing tongues, I managed to right myself and figure out how to hold the leashes as had been intended in the first place.

Aside from having to pick some gravel out of my elbow, nurse a sore shoulder for a few days, and scrape my pride from the street, I was fine. However, I learned an important lesson. Pay attention; don't just listen, but listen for understanding.

There are many places in the Bible where we are told to listen and pay attention to instructions from God.

First, when Jesus was baptized, God appeared in a cloud and said "This is my Son, whom I love; with him I am well pleased. Listen to him!" (Matthew 17:5 NIV).

Second, Jesus instructed people to listen and understand when He taught. "Jesus called the crowd to him and said, 'Listen and understand.'" (Matthew 15:10 NIV).

Third, when Jesus was helping his disciples understand his coming death, he said, "Listen carefully to what I am about to tell you; The Son of Man is going to be betrayed into the hands of men." (Luke 9:44 NIV).

Finally, if we belong to Christ, we will listen and follow his teaching. "My sheep listen to my voice; I know them and they follow me." (John 10:27 NIV).

Listening to God must be very important or it wouldn't have been stated repeatedly. How often have we thought, if not said to our children, "How many times do I have to tell you…?" Similarly, how many times does God need to tell us things before we listen to understand his instructions in the

Bible? Thankfully, God is patient with us when we fail and He gives us more opportunities to listen. We live in a world of sin and trouble, but when we follow his instructions, we have a better understanding of God's plan and that gives meaning and purpose to life.

By the way, in case you're wondering, the rest of the walk was event free.

WHO IS IN CHARGE?

On April 14, 2013 we began a 3 week trip. We planned our route, places to stay, people to visit, and gathered maps and contact numbers. We had everything under control.

Early on the 13th, we heard that a blizzard was heading our way so we called our April 14th destination and asked if we could arrive early. With that arranged we headed out and made our destination easily. The next morning however, a blizzard had gripped our world. By noon a day later than we planned, we headed out again. However, the driving snow caused engine problems so we had to back track to obtain a different car.

Following the icy path of the storm as well as coming upon an accident as we topped a hill added to the stress of our trip. Then, just as we came to the Colorado border we hit a second blizzard that closed the Interstate. Stranded motorists cluttered the area.

We finally reached our nephew's home south of Denver just hours before the beginning of a conference my husband wanted to attend. However, a couple of days later my nephew came in from the garage saying, "There's a lot of red fluid on the garage floor." Red fluid on a garage floor where your car was just sitting is never good! It was probably the result of that accident in Wyoming. So, repairs were needed.

After the conference we were rerouted again because of another cousin's unexpected surgery. We were just south of Duluth, Minnesota when we heard that a third blizzard was coming through. When we awoke on May 1 the ground was blanketed with snow. Fortunately, we were on the edge of this blizzard and were able to drive away from it in about 30 minutes.

When we were about 5 hours from home there was a sudden strange noise accompanied by difficult steering. Yes, a flat tire! We changed it and traveled slowly on the "limper" watching for a shop to get the original fixed. When we found a shop open (on a Saturday afternoon) they looked at the tire and said it was not fixable. It took us longer to get home on the spare but we finally did.

Did this trip go as planned? Not as we planned but I'm sure that it went exactly as God planned. Who knows what appointment he wanted us to make along the way? Who knows what God may have protected us from by delaying us? We will probably never know but one thing that has been engraved in our hearts and minds is this: "Now listen, you who say, 'Today or tomorrow we will go to this or that city, spend a year there, carry on business and make money.' Why, you do not even know what will happen tomorrow. What is your life? You are a mist that appears for a little while and then vanishes. Instead, you ought to say, 'If it is the Lord's will, we will live and do this or that.' As it is, you boast in your arrogant schemes. All such boasting is evil." (James 4:13-16 NIV).

Wherever we go and whatever we do, we can rest in the knowledge that God is in control. "The heart of man plans his way, but the Lord establishes his steps." (Proverbs 16:9 ESV). We must all remember this daily.

LITHUANIA

WHAT WOULD HAPPEN IF WE SERIOUSLY SOUGHT GOD?

"What would the Lord have to do if He wanted us to live somewhere else or do something else?" We have asked ourselves this question many times through the years. This has led us to some interesting glimpses of who God is and how much He cares for us.

Several years ago, for example, we held two teacher's contracts and had to decide which one to sign. We prayed, asking Him to show us what to do, but we did not see any "writing on the wall." Finally, as the deadline came, we sat down, prayed again and listed the pros and cons of each teaching position. We prayed that God would intervene if we did not choose according to His will. The next morning, in our daily devotional, the chosen scripture said, "I will instruct you and teach you in the way you should go; I will counsel you with my eye upon you." (Psalm 32:8 ESV). We looked at one another with tears in our eyes and shivers down our spines knowing that God had just answered our request for His leading. This gave us confidence that no matter where we are working or living, He will lead us if we ask Him. We still quote that verse and we continue to tell the Lord that we want to be where He wants us.

At one point, though we didn't know why, we felt the need to decrease our mortgage and living space and we wanted to get rid of lots of "stuff." Seeking God's leading He provided an older home which we bought, renovated and moved into. Our other house sold and our mortgage was cut in half. At the same time we attended a conference called "Finishers" (missionnext.org). This organization matches middle age to retirement age people who have established skills, with mission agencies who need those skills. At this conference, leaders from many mission agencies helped us sort out how we might serve in missions. As a result of that conference, we applied for positions at Lithuanian Christian College and were accepted. This college was established in 1991 after the breakup of the Soviet Union. Its purpose is to train strong leaders for Lithuania and surrounding nations. They offer majors in theology, business, English, psychology and sociology. Having "volunteer" instructors from North America controls the cost so that the college is not just for the elite. We were greatly blessed by those in our church as well as many others who supported us in this short-term mission trip.

My husband taught algebra and statistics classes. I worked in various offices, assisting in the production of their accreditation self-study book, creating faculty newsletters, and cataloging Business Department resources. I also prepared dinner for a weekly Bible study, led by the college chaplain, for 20-30 students who are new Christians or who wanted to know about Jesus Christ.

The changes we made in our financial status made it

possible to participate in a mission trip like this. Our time there was an eye opening blessing to spiritual needs around the world.

Now, what about you? Are you where the Lord wants you? Are you seeking His direction for your life? Have you ever asked, "What would the Lord have to do to get my attention if He wanted me in a different place?" He promises to lead and guide when we are willing to follow.

THE ONE WHO TRUSTS
GOD IS INVINCIBLE PART I

Religious persecution and oppression have been problems for people of faith since Bible times. (2 Corinthians 11). While in Lithuania, I did casual interviews of those who lived during the Soviet occupation. They told me of the fear driven control that began as soon as a child entered school. The youngest were called October children (based on the October 1917 revolution when communism began). Children were lined up, given pins and flowers. They were read poetry and as long as they did as they were told, they were treated well. Teaching and testing for loyalty continued as they were promoted to the next level: Pioneers. Again, pins and neck scarves were bestowed which were to be worn at all times. The third level, komsomolec, was entered around the age of 15 till around 28. During this time it was expected that leadership abilities, talents and loyalty to the Communist party would develop more fully. Passing this level successfully meant full Communist status, which resulted in better jobs and improved living conditions. If Communist teachings were followed and no traces of faith were ever demonstrated, life was good. Faith was a non-issue for those who didn't believe, but to those who did believe, Communist teachings resulted in constant tension.

Under Communism, everyone was watched. If someone was arrested, for any reason the government chose, family and friends of that individual were shunned to avoid suspicion. This resulted in lives of isolation.

After arrest, there was interrogation and perhaps death. In Lithuania and other nations such as the Czech Republic and Poland, six million died, half of whom were Jews. We visited one site where 30,000 Jews and 20,000 others were systematically tortured and shot. Fresh flowers in memory of those who died are still left regularly at this site. To say it was overwhelmingly unbelievable does not begin to convey the emotions that these sites evoke.

After these murders, hundreds of bodies were strewn naked in the fields and streets and everyone in town was lined up for a forced viewing. Anyone who exhibited any emotion was assumed to have recognized a son, daughter, husband, wife, parent or friend and might be shot on the spot or arrested and placed in a concentration camp for interrogation. It is little wonder that the people we met on the streets of this former Soviet bloc country had emotionless faces.

Priests, cardinals and nuns were among those arrested. The KGB titled Sister Nijole Sadunaite the most dangerous criminal in Lithuania. She did not mind this title and realized that even those lost in lies and terrorism recognize that there is a spiritual force. She believed that even the weakest person is invincible when relying on God. In 1974 she was arrested while working on an underground journal documenting the oppression. She survived and after the occupation she began a type of Salvation Army ministering to the physical, emotional and spiritual needs of the people. One can read more of her life in her book "A Radiance in the Gulag."

What would we do if we lived in these types of circumstances? Would we feel invincible? Would this drive us to the Bible to develop spiritual strength? Unknown life experiences may be ahead and the coming of the Lord could be at any time. "Therefore you also must be ready, for the Son of Man is coming at an hour you do not expect." (Matthew 24:44 ESV).

THE ONE WHO TRUSTS
GOD IS INVINCIBLE PART II

While in Lithuania in 2005 I learned that they had the highest suicide rate in the world. Years of oppression during the Soviet occupation greatly impacted their outlook on life. Below are glimpses into some of the impossibilities of life during that time.

One remembered: "If I was seen in church on Sunday I was ridiculed and shamed on Monday; first by my teacher then my classmates. My 'behavior' became a part of my permanent record. My parents sent me to live with grandparents in the country and there I was taken to church and taught about God. Our family was part of a silent resistance and my father taught me about our government leaders. He showed me literature that could have gotten us in a lot of trouble. He told me about those who hid in the woods living on mushrooms and wild berries, trying to rid the country of Communism. Once when a friend said that Stalin had given the Lithuanians freedom, I quickly disagreed saying that he had only replaced one occupation with another. She became very upset so I learned to keep my opinions to myself, but I always remembered the truth my family taught me."

Another person told of going 200 kilometers from home to have first communion. She said, "If I had celebrated first communion at home, I would not have gotten a recommendation to the University and my father may have lost his job or been deported. I remember that many of my relatives were deported to Siberia and never returned. Holidays were difficult. Sometimes authorities came to schools and asked small children nicely, 'Are your mommy and daddy having a Christmas party?' We learned early to keep secrets and celebrate Christmas quietly in the kitchen. Even a house lit differently on Christmas Eve would attract attention."

Another remembered an incident when she was five years old: "My grandfather died and the family gathered for the funeral. We all got in cars and went to the church but my uncle did not go inside. I found out later that he had a job with the Soviet government and if he had gone into the church, even for his own father's funeral, he might have lost his job and wouldn't have been able to find another. I also remember as a young teen my mother warning me not to go to church very often as this would cause trouble for me. As times became more difficult, I gradually I stopped going to church. When the Soviet occupation was over, a young priest started coming into the streets and making friends with us. He played ball and went roller-skating with us. He invited us to his home to use his pool table, which was a rare thing to have. Through this he was able to develop a relationship with us and then we discussed spiritual matters."

As seen by these events, those who led the Communist

occupation sought to eradicate God from the people's hearts and lives. One writer referred to the occupation period as a time of moral and spiritual genocide. As evidenced by the suicide rate, many Lithuanians no longer have a vision of what it means to have God in their lives. They have forgotten what one of their nuns said: "The one who trusts God is invincible!" Does a relationship with God empower us to walk with Him confidently while treasuring our faith in celebratory worship?

THE PRICE OF FREEDOM

"About fifty police raided a banned Protestant church and detained church members during Easter celebrations. Simultaneously, police raided the church's land and broke the caretaker's arm in a bid to force the church to give its land to the state. Following the raids reporters learned that the Prosecutor's Office intimidated and threatened children in a bid to force them to sign statements that they would no longer attend Christian services and that they were renouncing their Christian faith. Parents were also pressured to write statements that they would not teach their children about Christianity and warned that failure to comply could see them deprived of their parental rights. A state religious affairs official told reporters that 'the police simply have to stop the church's members from holding illegal religious meetings.'"

The above quote is from Forum 18 News, Oslo, Norway printed on May 5, 2006. This event occurred in Uzbekistan on April 30, 2006. While we were in Lithuania I knew a student who was from Uzbekistan and I asked her about this incident. She told me that she knows people from that church. This event stems from the fact that any religious gathering in Uzbekistan is to be registered or it is considered illegal. Her banned Methodist church had over 150 in attendance. With more and more pressure being placed on the people, they have divided their church into many house churches of 3-5 people. By meeting in homes they do not draw as much attention to themselves. She also told of an older man who was telling others about his faith in Jesus. Government police found out about it and broke into his apartment and beat him up. She was somewhat fearful of going home for summer break. The government had already been asking her mother questions about her; where she was and what she was doing. They have also questioned her and she feared they will question her more.

When we hear of situations like this, we must pray for those living under these conditions. When Independence Day approaches each year, we must remember and thank God for our great American freedoms. We may not always have these freedoms.

There is a more valuable freedom, however, which can never be taken away or controlled by any government. Consider the freedom described in these verses.

"In him and through faith in him, we may approach God with freedom and confidence." (Ephesians 3:12 NIV).

"…through Christ Jesus the law of the Spirit of life set me free from the law of sin and death," (Romans 8:2 NIV).

"Now the Lord is the Spirit, and where the Spirit of the Lord is, there is freedom." (2 Corinthians 3:17 NIV).

"But now that you have been set free from sin and have become slaves to God, the benefit you reap leads to holiness, and the result is eternal life." (Romans 6:22 NIV).

To better understand and appreciate this eternal freedom, read the book of John to discover this Jesus of whom the scripture says, "So, if the Son sets you free, you will be free indeed." (John 8:36 NIV).

FINDING MY WAY IN THE FOG

There were times while we were in Lithuania when the fog was so thick that even from my 7th floor apartment building, I couldn't see much of anything. For days at a time in the morning, at noon and even at night the city of Klaipeda, Lithuania was shrouded in thick, soupy fog. It covered the ship loading cranes on the coast of the Baltic Sea. It hid the nearby tall apartment buildings. Every day was gray, wet and dark. I heard that this was normal for fall in Lithuania, especially near the seacoast but I found it rather depressing at times.

During our lives there are days or even weeks at a time that seem gray and dark to our hearts and minds. We can't see God as clearly as we would like. Sometimes we feel that we cannot see him at all. When we feel lost, how then are we to live? "For we live by faith, not by sight." (2 Corinthians 5:7 NIV). When I leave my apartment in the morning, I must live by faith, believing the school where I work is still in its usual place even though I can't see it. When I head to the grocery store, I must also live by faith, believing it is still in its usual place even when I cannot see it from my apartment window. As I gather my bags to get groceries (they charge for them) and head toward the general location of the store, I eventually see its outline and am assured that it is indeed there. If I depended on sight alone, I would not go to school or to the store because I would think they were not there!

We may laugh at how silly it would be to live by sight alone in the midst of fog, but don't we sometimes live by sight alone in our spiritual lives. We often say that God is far away in the dark times of our lives. Is He really? He promises, "Never will I leave you; never will I forsake you." (Hebrews 13:5b NIV). When He makes promises like this, why do we think He is gone, just because it is dark?

How do we find God when He seems distant? I found the school and store in spite of the fog, by heading down the street in the usual direction. Therefore, our help when God seems distant, is found in drawing near to Him in the Bible and through prayer. The Bible promises, "Come near to God and He will come near to you." (James 4:8a NIV). If we head in His direction, as He instructs, we will find that He is in the usual place and He is waiting to show us the way in our dark times.

PLENTY AND WANT

"The Hilton truck is coming," the spotter yells excitedly as he jumps from his observation point and runs up and down the streets. Children stream from every house around gathering in eager lines along both sides of the road. There are other trucks that come but none are as coveted as the Hilton truck.

What do these children want from the Hilton truck? They want the food that it carries. They are the first to receive from this truck's bounty. Other trucks that come bring food that has already been picked over by one or two other groups.

Still confused? Let me describe this in further detail. The Hilton truck is the Hilton Hotel garbage truck and they are bringing all the food that was not eaten from table or kitchen. The houses from which the children come are made of metal and wood scraps scavenged from their surroundings. The road is the trail through the dump in which they live. This is life for some children in Ethiopia. There are no schools and no trips to the mall. There are no name brand shirts unless they happen to find one as they dig through the dump. And, they probably don't really care about a name. It is a shirt and they need covering or they might be able to sell it. Some people from these families may have very low paying jobs but usually every member of the family spends from morning till evening looking through the dump for something they can use, eat or sell. It takes the whole family working all day just to survive.

While teaching in Germany we met a family working in Ethiopia. In addition to teaching in an English speaking school, this family is seeking funding to provide an education for at least one local child from each family who lives in these conditions. Often that child can grow up to build a better life, not only for themselves but their whole family.

Most likely, those reading this do not know anyone that poor nor are they that poor themselves. Most likely, anyone reading this will not sit down to a dinner prepared from food that was gathered from a garbage truck. However, there are needy people everywhere and we all have the opportunity to demonstrate our faith by helping them. As Thanksgiving, Christmas or other special seasons approach, look around in grocery stores and you should see signs that indicate ways to get involved by donating food, helping serve meals or working in a homeless shelter. Pay attention to your neighbors. No matter what the season of the year, are there people in need down the street or just around the corner?

Through our involvement, we show how faith and works can mingle in an amazing way. "What good is it, my brothers and sisters, if someone claims to have faith but has no deeds? Can such faith save them? Suppose a brother or a sister is without clothes and daily food. If one of you says to them, 'Go in peace; keep warm and well fed,' but does nothing about their physical needs, what good is it? In the same way, faith by itself, if it is not accompanied by action, is dead." (James 2:14-17 NIV).

STUFFING A PILLOW
THROUGH A FUNNEL

What was it like teaching and living in Lithuania? Did you have any friends? What did you learn?

These are some of the questions we were asked after our return. Actually, trying to explain our experience is rather like attempting to stuff a pillow through a funnel. It can only be done a little at a time. However, some thoughts have begun to come together.

Living in Lithuania was a lot like living in my local city. Everyone got up, showered, ate breakfast, took their children to school, went to work, shopped and cooked dinner. Lithuanians have hopes and dreams for themselves and their families and they strive to make them come true just as we do.

We developed some wonderful friendships among those working and teaching with us at the school: Americans and Lithuanians. The Americans had exciting stories to tell about how the Lord led them to teach in Lithuania. While God was moving us to go to Lithuania, He was moving someone in New Jersey, another in California, two from Minnesota, and even one person from Germany. Indeed,

God is at work worldwide. We spent time with many friends talking about daily life, going to concerts and on outings together. We went to one another's homes for dinner and dessert. We miss them.

I learned that, just as anywhere, some members of our communities were Christians and some were not. For example, there are many students there who do not know anything about God or what He could mean in their lives (just like here) and some of them were openly hostile toward anything having to do with "religion" (just like here). On the other hand, there were students who fast and pray for their peers; that the Lord would show Himself to them (just like here). There are many who do not go to church at all, and others who worship with fervency and pray with tears over those who do not know the Lord (just like here).

Before this trip, I had a pretty narrow perspective of God's work worldwide. Of course, I had heard stories about God working in other places and I was impressed. However, now I can put hands, feet and faces on God's work. I saw the pain in people's eyes as they wept for other's needs. I saw the orphanages full of needy children. I saw the despair of those who made their homes near and in the dump because that was all they could afford. I saw the void in the eyes of those consumed by alcohol. I also saw the joy of the Lord filling many lives. I saw lives being changed through the work God was doing at the college in which we taught and worked as well as in the churches we attended there. I now have a clearer picture of the verse, "The earth is the Lord's and everything in it, the world and all who live in it; for he founded it upon the seas and established it upon the waters." (Psalm 24: 1-2 NIV).

GERMANY

TREASURING GOD'S WORD

"Papa, you're not at work," said Alma as she and her brother Aldo entered the kitchen.

"No, my darling," answered Papa. "Today is the day the books come so it will be a day of celebration with no school or work."

"Tell me about the books," said Alma as she crawled quickly into Papa's welcoming arms.

"Many years ago, John and Marge Sorgen came to live in our village," said Papa.

"They tell me stories about Jesus!" said Aldo.

"They put a bandage on my knee," said Alma.

"They have been kind to us," said Papa. "They tell us about Jesus but after today, since they are teaching us to read, we will also be able to read about Jesus!"

"Today is the day," exclaimed Aldo!

"Yes," said Papa, "but we must hurry so we are not late for the celebration!"

After eating, Alma and Aldo scampered to dress. They had never been to such an event before!

When they approached the airstrip everyone from the village was arriving, dressed in their finest. When the plane appeared everyone cleared the grass strip that had been carved out of the jungle. The plane came to a stop and the crowds gathered closely as a door was opened. John Sorgen prayed, thanking God for this amazing gift. One box was moved from the plane to a table. A tribal leader prayed and finally the box was opened. As the books were lifted out, everyone cheered. Then all was quiet as the tribal leader said, "This is the book of Genesis that tells about God creating the world and The Gospel of John that tells us about the life of Jesus." John Sorgen encouraged them to read these words every day and to pray that more of the books of the Bible in translation would soon be finished.

After a community meal there were more prayers and singing. Finally, every family was given their own copy and they took them tenderly.

The names above have been changed but the story is the same whenever those who have never had God's Word finally receive part of it. I've seen recordings of these celebrations and the joy is contagious. There are nearly two hundred million people in the world who have no part of the Bible and no work has even begun toward meeting that goal. When Wycliffe Bible Translators and other organizations who work on Bible translation enter a village for the first time, it is their goal to help the people with practical and health needs. While serving, they learn the language that has been spoken for generations and create an alphabet and eventually write the Bible in the language best understood.

We, in America, can't remember a time when we did not have Bibles so perhaps that is why we don't always treasure it as we should. The book of Psalms reminds us what our attitude should be toward God's Word. "How sweet are your words to my taste, sweeter than honey to my mouth."

(Psalm 119:103 NIV). "My soul is consumed with longing for your rules at all times." (Psalm 119:20 NIV).

Because we believe that everyone should have access to God's word, we joined Wycliffe Bible Translators whose goal it is to provide the Bible in the heart language of every people group of the world. We don't have translation gifts but we can help provide education for the children of those who can. That is what took us to Germany to teach in an international school for 7 years.

OUTWARD APPEARANCE
OR INTERNAL CONDITION

———————

Before we moved to Germany, a family graciously invited us to stay with them while we finished our preparations. One of the first days we were there I volunteered to sauté vegetables in olive oil while others were off doing household tasks. I placed the pan on the stove and then found an olive oil dispenser by the sink. This seemed like a strange place for olive oil, but this was someone else's kitchen and I was unfamiliar with my surroundings.

Still being unsure about whether this really was olive oil, I studied the bottle and its contents. It didn't seem like the right color; but then I noted that the glass was colored. Perhaps it was flavored oil. I rotated the bottle in my hands and noted that the viscosity seemed correct for oil. To be absolutely sure though, I shook a small drop onto the back of my hand and tasted it. Startled, I quickly grabbed a glass of water and rinsed my mouth because the olive oil bottle actually contained dish soap! No wonder it was by the sink! I chuckled as I considered what might have happened if I had begun sautéing the vegetables in dish soap! I scanned the kitchen again. Finally, I saw another olive oil dispenser in a corner by the stove; imagine that! This seemed like the right location. It also looked very much like olive oil but I was not going to be fooled so I gave this liquid the same taste test. Yes indeed! This was olive oil so I set to work.

Both bottles looked like olive oil dispensers, both were in the kitchen and both contained a liquid of similar thickness. Yet, inside they were vastly different products. I was deceived by outward appearance.

Jesus gave stern warnings to the teachers of his time who gave every outward appearance of being upstanding, religious citizens yet inside were not. Jesus described them this way: "Woe to you, teachers of the law and Pharisees, you hypocrites! You are like whitewashed tombs, which look beautiful on the outside but on the inside are full of dead men's bones and everything unclean. In the same way, on the outside you appear to people as righteous but on the inside you are full of hypocrisy and wickedness." (Matthew 23:27-28 NIV).

We also, desiring to appear spiritual, can dress in the right kind of clothes, go to church and say the "right" things so that we look good on the outside. However, we are not changed on the inside unless we've asked God to forgive our sins and change our hearts.

To gain a more complete understanding of God's plan to forgive and change us on the inside, take some time to read the gospel of John. This book explains how only God can change hearts through Jesus' sacrificial death and transform hearts by the power of the Holy Spirit. As we draw closer and closer to eternity with every day that passes, we must remember "People look at the outward appearance but the Lord looks at the heart." (I Samuel 16:7c NIV).

PRIDE AND HUMILITY

Some years ago as I learned new techniques for helping students who had learning disabilities I was personally challenged to consider pride and humility. I sometimes ran into questions while preparing lessons and determining the best interventions. Pride would tell me to struggle alone but humility would walk down the hall to those more experienced to ask for help.

What does the Bible say about pride and humility? Is pride a temptation with which Christians struggle? Can it affect our eternity? How can pride and humility affect our lives and the lives of others?

Many Bible references on pride are sobering. Some include "When pride comes, then comes disgrace." (Proverbs 11:2a NIV). "Pride brings a person low..." (Proverbs 29:23a NIV). "In his pride the wicked does not seek him; in all his thoughts there is no room for God." (Psalm 10:4 NIV). A verse contrasting pride and humility says "He mocks proud mockers but shows favor to the humble and oppressed." (Proverbs 3:34 NIV). Finally, one verse about humility says; "with humility comes wisdom." (Proverbs 11:2b NIV).

Jesus knew that pride is a temptation so he told a parable which paints a very clear picture of both. Jesus told of two men who went to the temple to pray. The people admired the Pharisee for his strict keeping of the law and the tax collector was despised because he cheated many people. In the temple the Pharisee proudly bragged about the rules he kept. The tax collector humbly begged God for forgiveness and mercy for his sins. Jesus spoke highly of the tax collector's honest, humble evaluation of his life. Jesus was not pleased with the prideful boasting of the Pharisee. "I tell you that this man (tax collector), rather than the other (Pharisee), went home justified before God. For all those who exalt themselves will be humbled, and those who humble themselves will be exalted." (Luke 18:14 NIV). Pride is not only an outward action but a heart attitude. If pride keeps us from coming humbly to God asking for forgiveness for our sin, we place ourselves in a deadly position eternally.

In addition to eternal consequences, if pride keeps us from accepting any kind of assistance (physical, emotional or spiritual), we rob others and ourselves of a blessing. Some are called to be servants and if we don't accept their service we deny God's call on their lives. Sometimes we mistakenly call this kind of pride, humility by saying, "I don't deserve this attention!" or "I can take care of things myself."

If we are too proud to accept counsel, our relationships with others deteriorate and our work is not God honoring. We hurt those closest to us and miss out on God's blessings of an improved relationship or work situation.

I've come to the conclusion that I can best help my students by humbly asking for help even when my pride tells me "No!" That will, in the long run, help my students the most and the attitude will be God honoring.

Therefore, what will mark our lives with the Lord and

those around us; pride or humility? "All of you, clothe yourselves with humility toward one another, because, 'God opposes the proud but shows favor to the humble.'" (I Peter 5:5c NIV). I would rather live under God's grace than his opposition.

HAVE YOU CHECKED FOR PARASITES RECENTLY?

When we first arrived in Germany during the fall of 2007, I noticed that some trees had unusual looking clusters in them. I wondered if they were gigantic nests. I couldn't imagine what kind of bird might use them because they were not like any nest I'd seen before.

Sometime later, I learned that those clusters were actually mistletoe; that little bit of parasitic plant we hang over a doorway at Christmas time! As this parasite grows, it burrows further and further into the nutrition system of the tree, drawing food and strength for what it needs for life.

If not pruned from the tree, preferably when young and before forming berries, each mistletoe plant can grow up to two feet in diameter. As it matures, it can damage the branch and could eventually take over the whole upper part of the tree. At that point, the original tree may be unrecognizable and weakened.

How does the mistletoe grow there in the first place? Birds search out this favorite food source when the berries appear and then drop seeds into various tree branches. In that way, they "plant" mistletoe. The more plants in a tree, the more birds hang around eating and the more seeds are planted.

There are parasites that can get into our bodies as well and absorb the nutrients intended for us. These usually enter our bodies by way of unclean water or food sources. For example, when a hookworm, enters our bodies it attaches to our intestines and lives from our blood causing a type of anemia. This anemia means that we begin to lack energy and health and cannot be as productive. If not medically treated, their growth and development in our bodies becomes a serious threat to us.

I believe that parasites can get into our hearts as well and slowly consume us; changing who we are. They enter our heart and mind as tiny seeds of discontent, doubt or tension rising from misunderstandings, misinformation or misguided priorities. These parasites attach and, if not removed, grow stronger and stronger as they permeate our lives. They can eventually manifest themselves in strong emotions such as jealousy, bitterness, despair, worry, fear or covetousness. These parasites weaken us and hinder us from bearing spiritual fruit since our energy is going toward feeding the parasite rather than serving God.

I'm fairly confident that if a parasite was found consuming a tree in our yard, we would do something about it. If we found ourselves with anemia because of a physical internal parasite, I believe we would rush to the doctor to get it out! Will we be as dedicated about asking God to prune spiritually draining parasites out of our lives? It might be that we rather like our parasites of anger and worry! How do we get rid of the parasites so we can bear fruit for God again? Only God can do that. "He cuts off every branch in me that bears no fruit, while every branch that does bear fruit he prunes so that it will be even more fruitful." (John 15:2 NIV). All we have to do is ask!

UNDERSTANDING THE BIBLE

One challenge during our first weeks in Germany was grocery shopping. Of course, I recognized the usual things like eggs, bread and milk. However, even while choosing milk, I shook the container a bit to make sure it didn't sound like buttermilk.

Pictures on packaging helped me find other items such as cereals and canned goods. I even found less obvious things such as Hefe (yeast) and Petersilie (parsley). However, there are still many items that puzzle me.

Of course, meats didn't have familiar English names. Therefore, I didn't always know whether I was buying something made to roast or made for stews or soups. We've had some meat that was mighty chewy as well as some that has been incredibly tender.

Now in our third year I'm starting to see things in the grocery stores that I never noticed before. I don't know how I could have missed what appears to be in plain sight. I believe it's partly because I've learned some of the language. I've also gotten used to the basics so that I can concentrate my energies on the less obvious items. Even though it is challenging, our need for nourishment keeps me going back to learn more of the language of the foods of Germany.

I've been thinking about this learning process in relation to our need to grow in our understanding of what the Bible really has to say. Some may say, "When I open the Bible and try to read, it's like a foreign language." That may be true! However, as we persist, the terms become more familiar and we begin to understand more and more. Sometimes we may find some incredibly tough passages which need to be left for later when we know better how to "cook" (process) them. We need to spend time getting used to the language of the Bible in order to be nourished by it.

The language of the world at Easter time includes concepts such as: bunnies, baby chicks, flowers, colored eggs, fashionable clothes, egg hunts, and Peeps. However, if we are truly going to understand Easter, we need to grapple with the meaning and application of Biblical concepts such as Jesus' death, resurrection and ascension. If you are not familiar with the Bible, spend time in each of the gospel books of Matthew, Mark, Luke and John, getting to know the basic facts of the life and death of Jesus. Then spend some time in Acts and read how the early church processed and lived out what happened when Jesus came to earth.

We can't give up going to the grocery store in order to obtain our physical food and we shouldn't give up going to the Bible for our spiritual nourishment. Sit down with your Bible often asking God for wisdom and the ability to enjoy good spiritual meals. "If you call out for insight and cry aloud for understanding, and if you look for it as for silver and search for it as for hidden treasure, then you will understand the fear of the LORD and find the knowledge of God." (Proverbs 2:3-5 NIV).

USING OUR SPIRITUAL
TOOLS CORRECTLY

A couple of times, while teaching in Germany we pretended to be tourists. During those trips we encountered "perfect" days with sunshine and a few puffy clouds. Some days were just a bit too warm making us stop to rest and have ice cream. Sometimes it poured.

During one especially heavy downpour, we were walking to a grocery store to get sandwich makings for our day's outing. We had umbrellas so one would expect that only our feet would get wet. Yes, one would expect that! However, when we got to the grocery store and I stepped into the coolness, I realized that, even though I had used an umbrella, I was soaked to the point that I could wring water out of my shirt. My husband was dry except for a bit around his feet. I dripped through the store getting what we needed.

As we walked back in a lighter rain, I finally figured out why I had gotten so wet. I wasn't holding the umbrella properly!! Yes, I'm a grown adult and should know how to use an umbrella! However, instead of holding the umbrella horizontally above me, I held it at an angle...like a grand lady shielding myself from the sun. In so doing, I was creating a very efficient water slide. I was not using that rain tool correctly!

Do we use the tools of our faith correctly? There are many tools such as the Bible, prayer, the church and the people in it. This set of tools work best when used together. Our textbook, the Bible needs to be read and studied regularly not only while in class. It also needs to be studied with other students.

Prayer guides our understanding of the Bible and enriches our relationship with God. Just as speaking with our spouse or friend only when we have an emergency is hard on the relationship, prayer should not be reserved only for emergencies or when we want something. Talking with God and listening to God are essential. We don't often think of spending time listening during prayer but isn't listening part of any conversation between friends? "You are my friends if you do what I command. I no longer call you servants, because a servant does not know his master's business. Instead, I have called you friends, for everything that I learned from my Father I have made known to you." (John 15:14-15 NIV).

Just as it's good to use an umbrella properly to avoid getting soaked, we benefit greatly when we properly use the tools God has given. "The law of the Lord is perfect, refreshing the soul. The statutes of the Lord are trustworthy, making wise the simple. The precepts of the Lord are right, giving joy to the heart. The commands of the Lord are radiant, giving light to the eyes. The fear of the Lord is pure, enduring forever. The decrees of the Lord are firm, and all of them are righteous. They are more precious than gold, than much pure gold; they are sweeter than honey, than honey from the honeycomb. By them your servant is warned; in keeping them there is great reward." (Psalm 19:7-11 NIV). "Do your best to present yourself to God as one approved, a worker who does not need to be ashamed and who correctly handles the word of truth." (2 Timothy 2:15 NIV).

TAKING FREEDOM FOR GRANTED

"It's a sad day in our country today! Please pray right now! The mobs are sweeping the country burning all the churches now. They just went through my neighborhood. Smoke fills the air. Now I hear that the mobs are demanding people to show them where Christians live. Many of the Christians were gathered at my school for a sports event this morning and cannot go home. They are sending me messages to come to safety of the school ground, but I can't drive out now. The street is in chaos. Almost all the churches in our region are burnt (except a few house-churches), and even the Christian schools were attacked and burned. I heard that the army was dispatched on request to protect our school campus and the adjoining Bible College. All the church services are cancelled tomorrow. Maybe due to crying and fasting all day, but now I have a terrible headache. Please keep those grieving their loss tonight in your prayer! I just received an email from the US Embassy warning us of their forecast of this disruption to escalate tomorrow and to last for a while. Our mission has warned us to be ready to leave on a short notice. Please continue to keep us in your prayers!"

Sometimes, in order to make a point, I make up stories. However, I did not make this up. I received the above correspondence from a missionary who worked in a closed area. Can we imagine living in the midst of such persecution? Can we imagine fearing for our lives because we are Christians? Is our faith strong enough to spend hours at a time fasting and praying for safety for ourselves and for those who live around us? Does our relationship with God mean enough to us that we would risk being killed in order to stand firm?

It may be easy for us to think that this could never happen in the United States. We live in a free country. Yes, right now, in my small city it is safe to go to church and speak what we believe. The worst that is likely to happen is that we might endure some teasing or ridicule for our faith. However, given recent world events, we must not become complacent but we must pray for our brothers and sisters who do live under such persecution. We must strengthen our own faith so that we are ready for whatever happens.

Finally, according to the Bible, how should we react to such trials? "Consider it a sheer gift, friends, when tests and challenges come at you from all sides. You know that under pressure, your faith-life is forced into the open and shows its true colors. So don't try to get out of anything prematurely. Let it do its work so you become mature and well-developed, not deficient in any way." (James 1:2-4 The Message). Now that's a challenge!

DON'T GIVE THE ENEMY
AN ADVANTAGE

I love homegrown lettuce. While I'm not a great gardener, lettuce is one of the things I plant in the spring. Unfortunately, besides a few flower pots on my patio in Germany, I had no place to plant a garden. I had heard that lettuce could be grown in pots so I tried it, again and again and again. I watched excitedly as the seedlings appeared; but a few days later they always vanished.

Being ever hopeful I tried one more time. I dug up the soil in a large pot, scattered the seed, lightly covered it and regularly watered it. Soon lots of baby leaves were popping out of the ground. I began dreaming of that salad I would have in a few weeks. However, one day I found that they had again vanished without a trace.

After a bit of frustrated investigation, I finally realized what happened. Snails also like lettuce! Given the amount of rain we have in southern Germany, we have an abundance of snails on my ground floor patio. Each time I tried growing lettuce, I provided soil, water and sunlight but I did not provide protection. I gave an advantage to an enemy of my lettuce by placing the pot of greens in the snail's living room!

Considering how I should protect my lettuce from its enemy, I planted seeds again, but this time I put the pot on my patio table hoping the snails would not know to climb the table legs. The plants are larger than I've ever seen them here. I'm still several weeks away from that salad I crave but I have hope.

Just as there are natural enemies of my lettuce plants, there is an enemy after our spiritual lives; our very souls. We must guard ourselves so that we are not consumed by that enemy. "Be alert and of sober mind. Your enemy the devil prowls around like a roaring lion looking for someone to devour." (1 Peter 5:8 NIV).

While Satan cannot defeat us, he will certainly try. In the end, Satan is going down and wants to take as many of us with him as possible. One of the ways Satan tries to take us down is in the lies he tells in order to spiritually discourage and paralyze us. Below are some of the lies Satan uses. Next to each lie is a Bible verse that provides an answer for each of those lies. First, God could never forgive you so don't even bother asking! (I John 1:9). Second, God doesn't care about you because you are too insignificant. (Matthew 10:29-31). Third, don't bother reading the Bible because it's hard to understand. (2 Timothy 2:15). Fourth, what's the big deal if you never pray? (Luke 21:36). Fifth, God is a God of love so he would never send someone to hell. (Matthew 25:41). Sixth, go ahead and do whatever you want; you can always ask forgiveness later. (Matthew 7:21). We must test every lie of Satan against the truth of the Bible.

The next time we sit down to have a salad, be it made with greens from the store or from our garden, we must remember that it was provided soil, water, sunlight and protection so that we could enjoy it. Let us provide the same nurturing and protection for our spiritual lives so that we can grow strong and mature in God.

SURPRISES IN LIFE

It was a brisk morning in September as I walked to school with my lunch in hand. Entering my office I remembered that the person who used this office before me often placed her lunch on the wide outside ledge to keep it cool. So I placed my fruit and sandwich outside, closed the window and began work. About half way through the morning I heard a tapping at my second floor window! I turned to see a giant crow pecking at my lunch! As I rose from the chair to scare him away he took flight alright, but with my sandwich, plastic bag and all, in his beak! I was surprised that a crow could actually do this. If I'd expected it, I would have walked to the end of the hall and placed my lunch safely in a refrigerator.

Then there was the evening that I went out on the patio to shake my dust cloth and stepped on a strangely soft lump. As I stepped back I saw a dead bird. I suppose the neighborhood cat who likes to sit on our patio thought this was an appropriate trade for use of the space! That surprise made me glad that I was at least wearing slippers! I will prepare for that possibility in the future by turning on a light before I head out after dark.

Some years ago, when our son had a newspaper route, my

husband went out to help with an extra day's worth of papers that came after a paralyzing blizzard. After retrieving papers from the car, he turned to head down the sidewalk only to slip on ice and break his ankle. Surgery including nails and pins quickly followed. That was a surprise that changed how our family did things for several weeks! Greater care or better foot wear might have prevented that accident.

I'm sure these stories have triggered memories of many surprises you've had. Some may have been good and some may have been bad.

One event that is coming for all and will surprise some but not others, is our first face to face encounter with Jesus. We don't know just how or when it will happen, but we are promised that it will happen. Jesus said, "Therefore keep watch, because you do not know on what day your Lord will come. But understand this: If the owner of the house had known at what time of night the thief was coming, he would have kept watch and would not have let his house be broken into. So you also must be ready, because the Son of Man will come at an hour when you do not expect him." (Matthew 24:42-44 NIV).

For some, our first encounter with Jesus will come as a result of a sudden, serious injury or accident such as a heart attack or stroke. For others our first face to face meeting with Jesus will be after a long, lingering illness or a natural ageing process. For others, his actual physical return may be our first face to face encounter with Jesus.

Let us not be caught off guard. All we need to know about preparing for this surprising encounter is written in God's life manual, the Bible. The next time you are surprised by something, be it good or bad, remember the future surprise of meeting Jesus. Don't put off making the necessary preparations.

We Might Fall When We Least Expect It

It happened when we were navigating the Paris subway and train system on our trip from the US to Kandern, Germany. I was carrying a bag containing two computers, a purse, a backpack with books and snacks and pulling two pieces of carryon luggage. My husband was handling four larger suitcases.

Everything was alright until the luggage tandem straps broke so that linking them together was no longer possible. Since luggage carts were not allowed on train platforms, my husband moved two pieces of luggage while I watched the two left behind. Then he returned for the other two while I watched the two he had just moved. Each time we arrived at an escalator I went ahead and he sent suitcases behind me so I could set everything aside. Then we started down another hall toward the train. While this was exhausting and slow, it was working.

Because I'm not so coordinated, I knew I had to be careful each time I got on an escalator. I purposefully arranged each piece of luggage I was carrying so that as the steps moved up, I would have everything balanced. Nearing our final train connection with little time to spare, I hastily entered the escalator thinking, "I'm OK since everything has been fine so far."

However, as the steps moved up I realized that everything was not *fine*. I tried desperately to pull things into balance in the midst of the crowd but it was too late and I tumbled backward. I don't remember more than momentary panic and then finding myself lying on my back, with my head down as the escalator continued its upward climb. Do you know how hard it is to get up from a position like that? (You have permission to laugh!) I found that it was too hard so I decided to lie there till it got to the top so I could get up from a flat surface.

However, someone pressed the emergency stop button. Now I had no choice. I tried rolling over but the luggage was in my way. A woman tried in vain to help. Finally a man walked down the steps and reached out his hand. With a mighty pull from each of us, I was again upright. Embarrassed, I gathered my luggage scattered on the steps and climbed to the top. Everyone watched till I was on level ground. I put on a brave smile and nodded my head assuring my French observers that I was fine. My husband grabbed two of our bags and raced up the stairs to check on my wellbeing. A bleeding elbow, sore shoulder and knee along with several bruises reminded me of this incident for several days.

My accident occurred because I got careless about possible hazards. This carelessness was rooted in the pride that I was doing so well.

Careless pride is also a dangerous thing spiritually. "Pride goes before destruction, a haughty spirit before a fall."

(Proverbs 16:18 NIV). Hazards (temptations) come our way all the time. Sometimes we are watchful but sometimes we get careless and that is when we fall. We have been warned: "So, if you think you are standing firm, be careful that you don't fall." (1 Corinthians 10:12 NIV).

Let's not get lazy in our Christian lives, especially if we've avoided falling for a while. That's when temptations might surprise us the most! "Watch and pray so that you will not fall into temptation." (Matthew 26:41a NIV).

WHEN THE LEANING
POST MOVES

As I placed the key in the car door, my heart sank. The dome light was on and we had not used the car for two days. The only response from the car was a weak groan. My husband came from our apartment just then and tried again. There was an even weaker groan and then it was silent.

Since we lived at the top of a slight incline and the car was not an automatic, it was possible to start the engine by coasting and releasing the clutch. David was already in the driver's seat so he put the car in neutral and it started rolling from the parking spot toward the street. I gave the car a bit of a push to encourage it to face down the incline. He put the car in first gear and it began rolling forward. I leaned into the car again to get it going a bit faster to ensure that it would start. As the clutch released, the car lurched, started and took off.

That happened very quickly. My reaction was not as quick! Therefore, the car that I was leaning into was suddenly gone. The forward momentum of my body caused me to flail my arms trying to stay upright but it was a losing battle and I crashed to the ground. One of our high school students was walking to school just then and he, having witnessed the whole embarrassing comedy, came over quickly asking if I was alright. Besides a bruised hand and incredible embarrassment, I was fine.

Later, after having a good laugh with other teachers over how that would have looked on a movie, I decided there had be a lesson. I was leaning on something that was not dependable and I knew it. After all, it was our purpose to start the car so that it would move away.

How often in our daily lives do we lean on that which is undependable? Do we lean on our relationships, prestige, intellect, positions, friends, children, money, or our own ability to keep us upright? Relationships change, prestige can be lost, and intellect can't fix everything. We can lose our position or friends. Children grow and move away. History tells us that money can be lost.

When we depend on anything other than God, we eventually find that what we leaned on fails us. We flail around grasping for something else before crashing in a confused daze. "Such is the destiny of all who forget God; so perishes the hope of the godless. What they trust in is fragile; what they rely on is a spider's web. They lean on the web, but it gives way; they cling to it, but it does not hold." (Job 8:13-15 NIV). We must remember that only God is strong enough to hold us up and keep us safe when hard times come.

Even though I understood what we were trying to accomplish that Monday morning, I didn't understand the result of my dependence on the car. "Trust in the Lord with all your heart and lean not on your own understanding." (Proverbs 3:5 NIV). I need to remember that "You (God) are my strength, I sing praise to you; you, God, are my fortress, my God on whom I can rely." (Psalm 59:17 NIV). Let's learn to lean only on what is proven to be dependable.

GOD PERFORMS
MIRACLES TODAY

The landscape in southern Germany where we taught often bursts with miracles in the spring. As we step out of our apartment or drive along the country side, we are overwhelmed by the dazzling yellow forsythia bushes, the magnificent magnolia blossoms and the lacy apple and cherry blossoms. They all demonstrate God's miraculous handiwork. Scattered through the Bible we find more miracles as we learn about Noah, Jonah and Abraham. We also read how Jesus fed 5,000 people with five loaves and two fish, healed the sick and even brought some back to life. He calmed raging waters and peoples' quaking hearts. As we consider these miracles, we could find ourselves wishing that God would show himself like that today. Sometimes, he does.

In a remote country some time ago there was a man I'll call Bill, who worked as a school administrator. One morning Bill awoke to loud knocking. When he opened his door he was met by two men with large guns. They had another administrator with them and said Bill was to join them. As the four of them took off on two motorcycles Bill's wife and two young sons gathered the community to pray for their safe return. While away, Bill and his co-worker were questioned intensely about a plan they supposedly had to overthrow the government. The captives truthfully and calmly denied the charges. After several hours, they were allowed to return home. There they found out that many prayed while they were gone. The local community knew that when the men on cycles come to take someone away, they "never" returned alive. God worked a miracle in the hearts of the captors that day.

At another time in a remote area of the world, a very large number of people gathered to hear someone speak about a man named Jesus. A huge tent had been erected and people crowded in since there was no sound equipment. Just as the speaker began it started to rain. It rained so hard that nothing could be heard above the thunderous sound of the rain on the tent roof. The pastor paused and prayed, "Lord, please stop the rain so that these spiritually hungry people may hear about you. Amen." In a few moments the rain did stop; but only over the tent! The downpour continued beyond the tent. So, with a captive audience, the speaker was able to tell about Jesus. Many became Christians that day.

I believe these stories to be true because I have spoken personally with those who experienced them.

While we must never view God as a magician, we must believe in his power if we are to grow in our understanding of his nature. If our God can stop the rain over a tent while it rains all around, can't he calm the storms of our lives? If he can stop cruel men from murderous plans, can't he protect us in dangerous circumstances? If he can rise from the dead, can't he also care for our children, give wisdom to doctors in difficult situations and care for our ravaged finances?

God assures us: "So do not fear, for I am with you; do not be dismayed, for I am your God. I will strengthen you and help you; I will uphold you with my righteous right hand." (Isaiah 41:10 NIV). No matter what difficult circumstances enter our lives today and in the weeks to come, we must never forget that we serve a God of miracles.

How Valuable Is Our Integrity?

While living in Germany I sometimes shopped at a store similar to Wal-Mart called Marktkauf which was about 30 minutes from our home. One day while shopping, I purchased groceries, household items and four small gifts that were to be part of a set. At home, while putting things away I discovered that one gift was missing. I was very disappointed and hoped that when I later returned to the store I could find a matching piece. Since it was small, I assumed that it had dropped out of my cart.

Later in the day, to my joy and consternation, I discovered the missing item in my purse! However, I wondered if I had paid for it. Checking out is a very rushed affair in Germany and I hoped that in my haste to bag my items it had just dropped into my purse. Scanning my receipt, I discovered that I had not paid for it! The item must have ended up in my purse as I filled my cart, inadvertently turning me into a shoplifter!!

What would you do? Some might say, "Well, I never meant to take anything and it is just a small thing. The store will never miss it." Others might say, "I just got something for nothing and I didn't get caught! Cool." Still others might say, "I just stole something and I need to make it right." I chose the latter response for the following reasons.

The dictionary defines stealing as: "Taking the property of another without right or permission." When I pay for a product at a store, in effect, I gain permission to take it home. The most obvious guidance in this situation is, "You shall not steal." (Exodus 20:15 NIV).

I understand that I could have gone to the store and try to explain what happened but with my limited German that would likely prove more confusing than helpful. But I had to make it right so later, when I made another trip to that store, I slid the item from my purse and placed it with the other items I was purchasing, paid for it and left.

Even if the store didn't know that I had taken the item, of course, God did. Years ago, I came upon someone in a store helping themselves to one band-aid from a box on the shelf to cover a sore heel. They then put the box back on the shelf and started to go on their way. Apparently I can't hide my feelings very well because after glancing at me they quickly returned to the shelf, put that band-aid box in their cart and walked away. Did they think I was spying for the store? I don't know, but the fact that I reacted to their actions appeared to change their behavior. Knowing God is watching us should affect our actions too.

Is there anything in our homes that is stolen? Are there pens from work, notebooks from school, a piece of wrapping, ribbon or some other paper? Is there tape or whiteout? The simplicity of the wording "You shall not steal," makes it all inclusive. It doesn't matter if the item is large or small, taken on purpose or accidently. Stealing puts our integrity on the line on earth and is known by God in heaven. "The man of integrity walks securely, but he who takes crooked paths will be found out." (Proverbs 10:9 NIV).

GOD STILL PERFORMS MIRACLES

Recently, students from Black Forest Academy (BFA) in Germany, where we used to teach, were planning their annual spring break service projects. Student groups had met several times planning practical helps for orphanages, schools, churches and homes for the needy. They investigated ways they could serve, what to take and what activities to do.

One week before departure, because of unrest in their African country, the decision was made to cancel that trip. It was a disappointment for that group after making so many plans. Thankfully, a similar opportunity was available in a different African country. However, with only a week left, it was going to be difficult to obtain visas. There wasn't enough time to mail requests for visas and even filling out paperwork online wouldn't fit into their time frame. They learned, though, that they could get the visas on time if they got them in person at an embassy. To do this, they needed 17 US $50 bills dated 2009 or later. Of course the German bank would have some US currency but the odds of finding 17 US $50's with the date restriction was slim.

The group decided to go to the BFA finance office to see if they had any ideas. "Just this morning," said the finance director, "someone came in to pay some of their child's bills. They brought in 27 US $50 bills. Let's see what we have." After retrieving those bills and examining each one, they found that *exactly* 17 were dated 2009 or later!

God knew where he wanted these students to serve. God showed the leaders and students that He can work miracles by planning in advance that a family obtain and pay with $50 dollar bills. God also made sure that the dates were correct on the exact number of bills that were needed. Talk about covering the details!!

There are some in this world who believe that God created us and flung us to the stars, walking away and letting us fend for ourselves. In the face of many stories like the one above, that opinion is unbelievable. Even more valuable is that a brief search of the Bible offers many examples of how God is actively engaged in caring for us. Consider Psalm 23 for example. This Psalm points out the many ways in which God, our good shepherd, cares for us. A good shepherd doesn't take the sheep to pasture and go home to watch TV for a while. Instead, he watches for predators who want lamb chops for dinner. He moves the sheep from pasture to pasture so that they have enough to eat. He leads them to quiet streams so they can drink safely. When danger arises He protects them. The picture that is painted here demonstrates someone who actively engages in our lives.

We are likely unaware of the many miracles that happen around us. Some become known and some may never be known. However, they do happen from time to time and that is a reminder that God is actively engaged in our lives and longs for us to take refuge, comfort and direction from Him because He will not forsake us. "For the Lord loves justice; he will not forsake his saints. They are preserved forever...." (Psalm 37:28 ESV).

HOME AGAIN

THE MORE WE OWN, THE MORE WE ARE OWNED

When we returned from teaching at Black Forest Academy in Germany we entered a new phase of our Wycliffe work from our Minot home. However, since we sold most of our possessions before leaving and since other possessions were stolen while we were gone and even though we were generously blessed by unexpected gifts, we needed to restock.

While considering what I owned, I found that I needed to seek God's perspective on my possessions. Are they a blessing or a curse? The following is some of what I found.

A wealth of possessions can cause problems in relationships. Two brothers, Lot and Abram (Genesis 13) traveled together until their possessions (flocks) became so great that quarrels started.

Those who have great possessions can become a desirable target for thieves. Especially throughout the Old Testament there are many stories of tribes of people being attacked and their possessions, including livestock, wives and children, being carried off.

We can lose our possessions and our very lives. In Numbers 16, Korah and his people and possessions were swallowed up by the earth as a result of their speaking against God's appointed leader, Moses. Similarly, in Luke 15, the prodigal son asked his father for his inheritance so that he could go out on his own. Eventually, the possessions were gone and this young man had no inheritance left.

Greed for more possessions and coveting honor from others can also cause problems. In Acts 5, Ananias and Sapphira lied about the amount of money they had received for the sale of land. They said they gave it all to the church but secretly kept some back. This deception cost them their lives.

There are some things more important than our possessions. In Second Chronicles 1, God commends Solomon for asking for wisdom instead of wealth, position and possessions.

In spite of the above negatives and cautions, possessions are also a blessing. "Blessed are all who fear the Lord, who walk in obedience to him. You will eat the fruit of your labor; blessings and prosperity will be yours. (Psalm 128:1-2 NIV).

When God blesses us generously with many possessions, we are to use our possessions to bless others. "If anyone has material possessions and sees a brother or sister in need but has no pity on them, how can the love of God be in that person?" (I John 3:17 NIV).

Our earthly possessions are nothing compared to the rewards available to Christians in heaven. In Hebrews 10, new Christians were instructed to joyfully accept the plundering of their property if it was taken because they were Christians, since greater blessings were coming.

The possessions we have are not really ours anyway, but God's. "For every animal of the forest is mine, and the cattle on a thousand hills. I know every bird in the mountains, and the insects in the fields are mine. Every beast of the forest is mine, the cattle on a thousand hills." (Psalm 50:10-11 NIV).

Therefore, our possessions can be a blessing or a curse. If we use them to help others and honor God they are a blessing to us and others. If we hoard them, stress over them or let them define our value, they can become a curse. Read Matthew 6:25-34 which tells us not to be anxious about our possessions. We need to carefully evaluate our perspective toward our possessions to decide whether they are a blessing or curse.

TRIPPING HAZARDS

In 2018 I received a new right knee. The morning after surgery I was expected to sit in a chair to eat breakfast and dress with the help of an occupational therapist. After that I walked down the hall and began to exercise the knee so that I could regain full use of it again. It was a challenge to bend my knee that had an 8 inch incision held together by 27 staples.

I soon recognized the many hazards in my environment that I had not noticed before surgery. Of course, I had been warned about the possibility of falling so I was told to remove all scatter rugs. I removed all but a large one in the living room and since it was so large, I didn't feel it would be a problem. However, it was that rug that was almost my undoing!

I noticed other hazards. I saw the dips and rises in parking lots. I noticed what seemed like boulders on gravel parking areas as well as simple things such as a pair of shoes by the door. The transition between carpet and hard flooring felt a bit like a deep drop off so I had to adjust my movement from one room to another. There could have been a temptation to stay in my chair where I felt safe. I would still be sitting there if I had not done the hard things like walking in spite of the fear, exercising in spite of the pain or asking for help when I really needed it.

This sudden awareness of hazards made me wonder about spiritual hazards we might ignore in our daily lives. I believe that just as I had to watch for tripping hazards and push harder after surgery, we need to do the same spiritually. Do these dips and rises in life weaken our faith or strengthen our resolve to follow harder after God by doing the work of studying and learning about Him? Do we trip over seemingly insignificant thoughts or comments and thus begin to doubt God's love and faithfulness? Are we frozen by the fear of moving from one place to another rather than seeking Him for a different way to make the transition? Do small annoyances become boulders because we refuse to pray over them or seek help when we need it? Do we keep something we should remove from our lives because we don't think it will be a real problem; in spite of the warnings?

Satan wishes to render us powerless by making us fearful and weak as he throws hazards in our path. "Be alert and of sober mind. Your enemy the devil prowls around like a roaring lion looking for someone to devour." (1 Peter 5:8 NIV). Instead, we are to "flee from all this and pursue righteousness, godliness, faith, love, endurance and gentleness. Fight the good fi ght of the faith…" (1 Timothy 6:11-12a NIV).

We don't want to be like those in the sadly funny videos that show people busily texting, who fall into pools, run into poles, trip on stairs, walk into walls or knock people down. They are not focused on potential hazards but are only inwardly focused. Let's be God focused!

Being Anchored to a
Firm Foundation

"Is that patio table and chairs for sale," I asked? "Yes, it is," said a person overseeing the estate sale. My husband and I looked it over, asked the price and determined that it was fair.

After paying we loaded the table on the back of our S-10 pickup. Then we added four chairs by setting each chair seat on the top of the table so the legs stuck up and the chair backs slid down into the pickup box. The person from whom we purchased the unit brought some shrink wrap and wound it around the chair legs. A few blocks down the road I saw the whole pile shift because of the wind created by our forward motion. My husband got out and discovered that two table legs had slipped into the joint between the pickup bed and the open end gate. All was well and perhaps more secure since two table legs were firmly in place. Confidently we continued toward home.

A few blocks later, startled by a loud crash, we saw the unit of chairs fly off the table and bounce onto the street. Thankfully, no one was behind us since they or their car might have been damaged! Also thankfully, the chairs seemed fine even though they had bounced into one another as well as onto the street. We determined that, even though this was a used set, it was sturdy! We returned them to their place on the table, anchored them together and then found a way to anchor the chairs to the table. The rest of the trip home was uneventful.

While no illustration is perfect, I felt there was a lesson to be learned that could apply to our relationship with Christ, other Christians, and the world. Being part of the church is twofold. First, we are to be anchored to Christ and second we are to live in unity with one another. Considering our little accident, I thought of it this way. It is important that we, the members of the church (chairs) are firmly anchored to Christ (the table). If we are not securely bound, we may be spiritually injured if we fly off when the winds of change bring challenges.

A problem can also occur if we are more tightly bound to each other than Christ. If we fly from our anchor in Christ, we could drag others with us into directions that could be harmful not only to ourselves but to them as well. We can even bring about confusion in the broader community if they are in our path. When the winds of oppression, change, challenge or dissention threaten to blow the body of Christ about, we can stay secure only if we anchor ourselves firmly in Christ.

Let us all be mature within the church by being firmly anchored to Christ. May we also be joined in unity with one another. "…so that we may no longer be children, tossed to and fro by the waves and carried about by every wind of doctrine, by human cunning, by craftiness in deceitful schemes." (Ephesians 4:14 ESV).

TRUTH AND GOD; IS THERE REALLY ONLY ONE WAY?

There are several routes from north to south in the city in which I live, Broadway being most used. If there is construction, other options include 3rd, 6th or 16th Streets or even the bypass around the city. During a massive flood in 2011, the bypass had constant use.

There are several ways to cook hamburgers. We can fry, grill or boil them. Boiling a hamburger might sound awful but while in my first year of college, I rented a sleeping room with kitchen privileges. I was not allowed to use the oven or fry anything and it was before microwaves (gasp), so boiling the meat was my only alternative.

There are various ways to accomplish many tasks but my question is: how many ways are there to God? Some think that there are several. The Bible says there is one.

"Salvation is found in no one else," (only Jesus) "for there is no other name under heaven given to mankind by which we must be saved." (Acts 4:12 NIV). Also consider; "Jesus answered, 'I am the way and the truth and the life. No one comes to the Father except through me.'" (John 14:6 NIV). Jesus did not say that he was one of many ways but he clearly says that he is the way. We also have the verse: "For there is one God and one mediator between God and mankind, the man Christ Jesus." (1 Timothy 2:5 NIV). Has the idea of one way to God ever caused a dilemma for you?

From my limited study of other religions only the Christian religion states that salvation is through Jesus Christ alone. I've heard it said that there are many men who would be god but only one God who would be man. Christianity is the only world religion in which God became a man to come to earth to die for us. It's true that there are many denominations within the Christian faith but accepting Jesus as the way of salvation needs to be the foundation of them. If we say we are Christ followers (Christian) we have to believe what Jesus, through the Bible, teaches. If we claim to be a Christian, we can't believe there are other gods or other ways to God since that contradicts Jesus very own words.

Why do we want to believe that there are many ways to God? Perhaps it is because it takes the pressure off of us to obey and allows us to create our own rules and our own truth rather than following God's truth that there is only one way to him.

Believing there are multiple truths is not new. Even during Jesus' trial, his truth was challenged. "You are a king, then!" said Pilate. Jesus answered, 'You say that I am a king. In fact, the reason I was born and came into the world is to testify to the truth. Everyone on the side of truth listens to me.'" (John 18:37 NIV). The word truth, as it relates to who God is, can be found nearly 100 times in the Psalms and New Testament. Do a search or scan pages looking for the word 'truth' to determine whether there is indeed only one way to God and God's truth. "Then you will know the truth, and the truth will set you free." (John 8:32 NIV).

BE READY FOR THE LURE OF TEMPTATION

"Congratulations!" said the voice on the phone. "You've won $400,000 and a new BMW. What are you thinking right now?"

"I have won a few little things through the years," I said, "but, who is this and how am I supposed to have won these things?"

"Your dreams are coming true today," said the voice. "Why are you so hesitant?"

"Well," I said, "I'm skeptical because I expect that sooner or later you'll ask me for personal information."

"No, I don't need personal information," continued the voice. "I tell you, I'm honest. As a matter of fact, the truck with your car and cash just left a nearby town on its way to you. You only need to pick up the voucher to receive the car and money."

"Really," I said hesitantly.

"I promise you that this is the best day of your life," he said. "I'll stay on the line with you and help you with the whole procedure at the grocery store. Have you dreamed of starting your own business?"

"Actually," I said, "my husband and I are missionaries...."

"Isn't that amazing," he continued. "I'm a pastor myself! Just think of all the ways this money can help you."

Next the voice told me that I needed to "process 199" to receive the voucher. He never used the word "dollars" and refused to call the "process" a transfer of money. Then he said that I needed to find Western Union. I asked why I needed Western Union if there was to be no fund transfer. He insisted that the transfer was not for the car but for the voucher to get the car. I hung up.

The above is an example of temptation's lure to have it all! Everyone is tempted. Jesus himself was tempted to turn stone to bread when he had not eaten for 40 days. He was tempted to jump off a high cliff to prove that the angels would protect him. He was tempted to bow to Satan and then Satan would give him the whole world to rule. Jesus responded with scripture such as: "'Away from me, Satan! For it is written: 'Worship the Lord your God, and serve him only.'" (Matthew 4:10 NIV).

We are warned that temptation will be lurking everywhere. "But if you do not do what is right, sin is crouching at your door; it desires to have you, but you must rule over it." (Genesis 4:7b NIV).

Jesus named the source of temptation. "Be alert and of sober mind. Your enemy the devil prowls around like a roaring lion looking for someone to devour." (1 Peter 5:8 NIV).

Yet, each temptation we face is not unique nor does temptation leave us helpless. "No temptation has overtaken you except what is common to mankind. And God is faithful; he will not let you be tempted beyond what you can bear. But when you are tempted, he will also provide a way out so that you can endure it." (1 Corinthians 10:13 NIV).

Just as Jesus used the words of the Bible to conquer his temptations, we must know the Bible well enough so that it can be an effective tool in the face of temptation. Just as we exercise our bodies and minds to improve our health we need to exercise our spiritual knowledge through Bible study so that we can use the Bible's tools. Then when temptation comes, we are armed and ready for the attack.

PATIENCE

I was standing in a check out at a local store when someone I know called, "I have such a hard time waiting in line! I have no patience. Write your next devotional on patience!"

I decided to take this individual seriously and did a short study on "patience." I found that, as God's children, patience is one of many attributes that we should be wearing in our lives. "Therefore, as God's chosen people, holy and dearly loved, clothe yourselves with compassion, kindness, humility, gentleness and patience." (Colossians 3:12 NIV).

After more study, I found that patience is a fruit of the Spirit that should be growing. "But the fruit of the Spirit is love, joy, peace, patience, kindness, goodness, faithfulness." (Galatians 5:22 NIV). The question is, "How do we obtain this fruit so that we might put it on?" Two examples come to mind.

First, if I plant seeds in a garden and expect "fruit", it is necessary for me to do something after the seeds are in the ground. I need to water, weed and fertilize. I generally need to tend the plants faithfully or the fruit will be poor in quantity and quality.

In our daily lives, we need to tend the salvation given freely by God to those who accept it on His terms. We need to follow God's commands to read the Bible not just to gain facts, but to gain understanding and grow in our love for God. We should read while asking questions such as, "What does that mean?" and "How is God showing His love here?" and "How should I apply that to my life?"

Second, let's pretend someone is living the life of a couch potato and then decides they want to improve their health by becoming a runner. They, too, should have a realistic plan. If their plan is to run a mile they shouldn't try that on the first day or they would give up before they start. They should gradually extend their distance and speed until they reach their goal of a mile.

The same is true of developing the fruit that God wants to grow in our lives as we follow Him. First, we need to tend that beginning fruit, giving it the nourishment it needs. We must feed our minds on the Word of God, seeking to know more about God so that we can become more like Him and reflect His character. Similarly, we strengthen our spirits by talking with God in prayer. When opportunities arise for us to exercise that fruit, we need to do the work with persistence and discipline.

The next time we're standing in line at a store, waiting for traffic to move as it should, waiting for someone to return the call they promised to return, or waiting for someone to make a decision, use it as an opportunity to exercise patience. We need to ask the Lord to fill our hearts and souls with His peace and a focus on others' needs. We need to ask the Lord to give us His patience so that we might reflect the Lord's love to others. Use waiting time to pray for others. Don't waste time and energy over things that cannot be controlled. "Be very careful, then, how you live--not as unwise but as wise, making the most of every opportunity, because the days are evil." (Ephesians 5:15-16 NIV).

FORGIVEN IS A WONDERFUL PLACE TO BE

Some memories are wonderful. I remember a special birthday party my mother planned for me when I was in grade school. Even though my birthday was in December, she used my favorite tablecloth that had robin's nests with little blue eggs in them. The fabric had silver threads through it and was splashed with delicate pink flowers. I remember warm summer days on the farm with the lake sparkling in the sunshine and a gentle breeze brushing through my hair. I remember stories my Mom read to me and I can still feel her gentle hand tirelessly rubbing my back when I couldn't sleep. I remember entering high school and the giddiness I experienced when I was invited on my first real date to the prom!

Some memories, on the other hand, are uncomfortable. I remember, at the age of five, hitting another girl because I was trying to please others. I remember lying to stay out of trouble or pouting in order to have my way. There are poor parental choices I wish I could change. I remember unkind things I've said.

These unpleasant memories sometimes flood my mind as I sing songs that speak of Jesus' suffering, the pain on His face, the burden of the cross on His back and the wounds in His hands. At those times, some of my uncomfortable memories flash through my mind with the specific label "sin" on them. I realize afresh that hitting the other girl was sin for which Jesus died. Lying to my mother was sin for which Jesus died. A selfish parental choice or hurting someone's feelings was sin for which Jesus died.

How often do we think of our specific sins? It is easy to speak of our sins in a very general way but I think by doing that we lose some of the impact of why Jesus came and what He came to forgive. Perhaps when we do think of specific sins, they are often someone else's REALLY BIG sins, not our "little" ones.

God doesn't differentiate between big and little sins. Sin is sin and needs to be called sin. It is only through Jesus that we can be forgiven of those sins. "Salvation is found in no one else, for there is no other name [Jesus] under heaven given to men by which we must be saved." (Acts 4:12 NIV). When we confess our sins we have assurance of forgiveness. "If we confess our sins, he is faithful and just and will forgive us our sins and purify us from all unrighteousness." (1 John 1:9 NIV). The assurance of forgiveness is sure! "For as high as the heavens are above the earth, so great is his love for those who fear him; as far as the east is from the west, so far has he removed our transgressions from us." (Psalm 103:11-12 NIV).

There may be natural consequences to some of our sins but only through Jesus can the guilt be taken away. We can enjoy our good memories and find forgiveness for our sinful memories. Forgiven is a wonderful place to be!

WHAT WE'VE INHERITED

We often look at children to identify characteristics inherited from their parents. We evaluate eyes, body build and skin tones. Once we get to know them, we also see their temperament. We even say things such as "he is his father's son" or "she looks just like great grandma".

Because I am adopted I really don't know what I inherited biologically. There must be a tendency to be rather short though! Research can even evaluate our genes to find out whether we've inherited a propensity toward particular forms of cancer or other diseases. We cannot be given a pill that will take that inheritance away, but we can be on guard concerning what that might mean for our future health.

There is something else we've inherited. When Adam and Eve were in the Garden of Eden, they were told not to eat a particular fruit. They chose to disobey, thus taking on sin that all future generations would inherit.

That inheritance is confirmed in I Peter 1:18 (ESV) which we'll look at piece by piece.

First, "...knowing that you were ransomed from the futile ways inherited from your forefathers..." Ransomed means "to obtain the release of (a prisoner) by making a payment demanded." There was a debt owed to God (futile ways) because of the disobedience and it has been paid. Was the payment money? No, because the verse next states, "… not with perishable things such as silver or gold…" In other words, no amount of money given to the church or a charity will buy the needed ransom. The verse concludes with how this ransom was paid: "…but with the precious blood of Christ, like that of a lamb without blemish or spot."

Until Jesus came to earth, God provided a temporary process for obtaining forgiveness of sin. This is described in the Old Testament books of Leviticus and Numbers. While the details of those books can be a bit overwhelming, there is a clear message that the blood of lambs or other animals was a temporary ransom for sin; "and the priest shall dip his finger in the blood and sprinkle part of the blood seven times before the Lord…" (Leviticus 4:6 ESV).

With the coming of Jesus, we can have a guaranteed inheritance. "In him you also, when you heard the word of truth, the gospel of your salvation, and believed in him, were sealed with the promised Holy Spirit, who is the guarantee of our inheritance until we acquire possession of it…" (Ephesians 1:13-15 ESV).

The sacrificial gift is offered but a gift not received is of no value. If I said I had $100 for the first person who came to my house with this book, it would only be valuable for the person who came to accept it. (I don't have that so please don't try it!) But, God asks us to accept his gift and he has something to offer that is far more valuable than $100! "…having the eyes of your hearts enlightened, that you may know what is the hope to which He has called you, what are the riches of his glorious inheritance in the saints." (Ephesians 1:18 ESV). Go to God to accept the eternal inheritance of heaven that He offers.

"Be still and Know that I am God"

They roamed the prairies trying to find enough "chips" to keep a fire burning in the sod shanty. They walked the frozen whiteness, searching for tracks that would hopefully lead to food. The tenacity of the early pioneers challenges me. I've sometimes wondered how they would react if they were suddenly transplanted to our times. I'm sure that initially, it would be frightening. We travel at break-neck speeds. We communicate instantly with people half way around the world. It doesn't matter if we are in our homes, at work, walking down the street or driving in our cars; we have access to incredible communication devices.

When we consider the technological advances over the last 100 years, they are truly amazing. However, one thing that strikes me is the fact that all these devices make noise. We seldom live in silence. When do we think? When do we listen to the quiet voice of God? Perhaps we even read our Bibles with music in the background.

Now, don't get me wrong, I truly love music and it's a vital part of our worship. Being part of the music team in our church is one of the highlights of my week. I enjoy a good TV program. I love listening to books on tape. But I sometimes find myself bombarded with so much noise, that I never have time focus on listening to God and He agrees. "Be still before the LORD and wait patiently for him." (Psalm 37:7a ESV).

Jesus understood the need for quiet when He said to His disciples, "Then, because so many people were coming and going that they did not even have a chance to eat, he said to them, 'Come with me by yourselves to a quiet place and get some rest.'" (Mark 6:31 NIV).

David creates a picture of finding God's comfort when he writes: "He makes me lie down in green pastures; he leads me beside quiet waters." (Psalm 23:2 NIV).

We can face our difficulties with quietness: "The LORD will fight for you; you need only to be still." (Exodus 14:14 NIV).

We can hear His voice best in the stillness: "Be still and know that I am God." (Psalm 46:10a NIV).

Silence before Him, is honoring to Him. "But the Lord is in His holy temple; let all the earth be silent before him." (Habakkuk 2:20 NIV).

Of course, God can speak to us in the midst of noise, but considering the above verses, it can be helpful to turn off the TV or music and spend an hour in silence. Use some of that silence to meditate on God's Word and part of it, just doing things around the house or at work. God is waiting to help us understand His presence, for He says, "The Lord your God is with you, the mighty warrior who saves. He will take great delight in you; in his love he will no longer rebuke you, but will rejoice over you with singing." (Zephaniah 3:17 NIV). Who can turn down an invitation to hear God sing in the silence?

WHAT WOULD YOU PUT
IN YOUR OBITUARY?

Someone told me recently about an unusual assignment he was given in a graduate school leadership course. Write your obituary! At the time he was in his 20's and his obituary was the farthest thing from his mind. However, it was required so he began gathering thoughts. He listed the money, possessions and status he hoped to achieve during his life time. But then he realized that character qualities might be more important. After all, most tombstones don't say, "Owned a Lamborghini and two businesses." When a tombstone has more than name and dates, it is often describes something about character such as, "Devoted Husband, Father and Grandfather" or "Loving Wife."

As I thought about his assignment myself, I wondered if there were examples of obituaries in the Bible. I found many in Hebrews chapter 11. This is often called the faith chapter since it lists many ways people's strong faith helped them get through life and helped them accomplish great things for God. Here are a few examples.

God spoke well of Able's offering because he gave of his first fruits. Being warned by God, Noah obeyed and built an ark according to God's direction. Moses' parents hid him because they could tell that he was special and they were not afraid of the king. Abraham headed off by faith, to a new land because God promised an inheritance for his people. Sarah, long past child bearing, did give birth to a son because she knew that God was faithful. After that, Abraham was even willing to sacrifice that only son, Isaac, because he trusted God completely!

Thinking about obituaries and faithful lives was prominent in my mind after my mother went home to be with Jesus at the age of 97. Some years ago she sought to help us write her obituary by listing some pertinent things about her birth, family, marriage and church membership. As we prepared for the funeral, however, we added details about her faith since that was such a defining part of her life.

As the sympathy cards arrived, we could see that others had also seen her live out her faith. One card from Kathy particularly painted a vivid picture of her character. When their family moved to the area, Kathy joined me in grade school. My mom and dad went to their home to welcome them to the neighborhood and invite them to church. During my childhood, whenever a new family moved to our rural area, Mom was one of the first to extend an invitation to church. Therefore, we picked Kathy up for church and Sunday school every week for many years. In her sympathy card, Kathy described that she will always be grateful that my parents picked her up since it marked the beginning of her spiritual growth. Other comments on cards referred to Mom's love and passion for others. Some spoke of her warm hand shake, snug hug and her bright smile born out of her faith. I am grateful for this legacy and challenged by my mother's example of Godly faithfulness.

Therefore, if we had to write our obituary, what would we include? Do we need to change our focus in life now so our obituary reflects what is most important when God calls us home? Will we leave behind a legacy of a character built on faith in God?

CPSIA information can be obtained
at www.ICGtesting.com
Printed in the USA
LVHW091153240121
677328LV00002B/415

9 781973 683605